Second Edition

# GREAT JOBS

# FOR

# Biology Majors

Blythe Camenson

D0290127

## VGM Career Books

Chicago  New York  San Francisco  Lisbon  London  Madrid  Mexico City
Milan  New Delhi  San Juan  Seoul  Singapore  Sydney  Toronto

Camen

- Great jobs for biology majors / Blythe Camenson. — 2nd ed. / rev. by Josephine Scanlon.
    p.    cm.
Includes bibliographical references and index.
ISBN 0-07-140898-3
1. Biology—Vocational guidance.    I. Scanlon, Josephine.    II. Title.

QH314.C35    2003
570'.23—dc21                                                          2003050180

2 3 4 5 6 7 8 9 0    FGR/FGR    2 1 0 9 8 7 6 5

ISBN 0-07-140898-3

Series design by Jennifer Locke

McGraw-Hill books are available at special quantity discounts to use as premiums and sales
promotions, or for use in corporate training programs. For more information, please write to the
Director of Special Sales, Professional Publishing, McGraw-Hill, Two Penn Plaza, New York, NY
10121-2298. Or contact your local bookstore.

This book is printed on acid-free paper.

# Contents

# Acknowledgments

I would like to thank the following professionals for providing insights into the world of biology careers:

Steven Bailey, curator of fishes, New England Aquarium, Boston

Rick Darke, curator of plants, Kennett Square, Pennsylvania

Leon Fager, Threatened and Endangered Species Program manager, U.S. Forest Service

Michele Graham, biology lecturer, Cal-State Hayward University, Hayward, California

Sharon Grata, medical laboratory technician, Johnstown, Pennsylvania

Susan Kelley, curatorial associate, Jamaica Plain, Massachusetts

Mary Lee Nitschke, animal behaviorist, Animal School Pet Behavior Services, Beaverton, Oregon

Carin Peterson, animal curator, Austin Zoo, Texas

Carla Lee Suson, micro/molecular biologist, Kingsville, Texas

Heather Urquhart, diving aquarist, New England Aquarium, Boston

# Introduction

## Biology: A Diverse Degree

People who become biology majors are as diverse as the wide variety of specialized fields in the biological sciences. And though the number of people entering biology careers each year is growing rapidly, so is the number of new fields being added to the list of options.

With so many possibilities available, new biologists will never feel pigeonholed. They can choose a career path suited to their personality and preferred lifestyle. For indoor types there are positions in labs, offices, hospitals, classrooms, museums, and libraries. Those who prefer the out-of-doors can opt for fieldwork at sea, in a tropical rain forest, a botanical garden, zoo, or aquarium.

Biologists can choose what kinds of systems or groups to focus on as well as the setting in which they work. With a degree in biology you can investigate a particular type or group of organisms, such as animals, bacteria, or plants. Or, you could work with a particular system within an organism, such as cells, tissues, or entire organs.

You could also investigate the interaction between organisms and their environment in a particular area, such as an ocean or a desert. Or you could focus on the chemical, physical, or medical aspects of living things.

Although many biologists are mainly involved in research and development and work in the laboratory or field, you can also find many other sectors of science to work in. There are jobs available in areas such as management, administration, service work, sales, writing, illustrating, and photography.

Biology majors can also use their undergraduate degrees as a stepping-stone to graduate work and then careers in university education, medicine, law, and advanced research. A biology degree offers great flexibility.

## The Road Ahead

In Part One of this book, you will learn many valuable tips on the job search, especially how to prepare and present yourself for the ideal job you are seeking.

In Part Two, you will explore a variety of career paths, many that are open to any biology major, some that are more defined, and still others that require further education or training, master's degrees, and often doctorates. Chapter 5 will give you a broad overview of the various paths; the remaining chapters will help you narrow those paths.

Once you've found the path you want to follow, you'll realize how important your biology degree is in reaching your ultimate destination.

# PART ONE

# THE JOB SEARCH

# 1

# The Self-Assessment

Self-assessment is the process by which you begin to acknowledge your own particular blend of education, experiences, values, needs, and goals. It provides the foundation for career planning and the entire job search process. Self-assessment involves looking inward and asking yourself what can sometimes prove to be difficult questions. This self-examination should lead to an intimate understanding of your personal traits, your personal values, your consumption patterns and economic needs, your longer-term goals, your skill base, your preferred skills, and your underdeveloped skills.

You come to the self-assessment process knowing yourself well in some of these areas, but you may still be uncertain about other aspects. You may be well aware of your consumption patterns, but have you spent much time specifically identifying your longer-term goals or your personal values as they relate to work? No matter what level of self-assessment you have undertaken to date, it is now time to clarify all of these issues and questions as they relate to the job search.

The knowledge you gain in the self-assessment process will guide the rest of your job search. In this book, you will learn about all of the following tasks:

- Writing résumés and cover letters
- Researching careers and networking
- Interviewing and job offer considerations

In each of these steps, you will rely on and often return to the understanding gained through your self-assessment. Any individual seeking employment must be able and willing to express these facets of his or her personality

3

to recruiters and interviewers throughout the job search. This communication allows you to show the world who you are so that together with employers you can determine whether there will be a workable match with a given job or career path.

## How to Conduct a Self-Assessment

The self-assessment process goes on naturally all the time. People ask you to clarify what you mean, you make a purchasing decision, or you begin a new relationship. You react to the world and the world reacts to you. How you understand these interactions and any changes you might make because of them are part of the natural process of self-discovery. There is, however, a more comprehensive and efficient way to approach self-assessment with regard to employment.

Because self-assessment can become a complex exercise, we have distilled it into a seven-step process that provides an effective basis for undertaking a job search. The seven steps include the following:

1. Understanding your personal traits
2. Identifying your personal values
3. Calculating your economic needs
4. Exploring your longer-term goals
5. Enumerating your skill base
6. Recognizing your preferred skills
7. Assessing skills needing further development

As you work through your self-assessment, you might want to create a worksheet similar to the one shown in Exhibit 1.1, starting on the following page. Or you might want to keep a journal of the thoughts you have as you undergo this process. There will be many opportunities to revise your self-assessment as you start down the path of seeking a career.

### Step 1    Understand Your Personal Traits
Each person has a unique personality that he or she brings to the job search process. Gaining a better understanding of your personal traits can help you evaluate job and career choices. Identifying these traits and then finding employment that allows you to draw on at least some of them can create a rewarding and fulfilling work experience. If potential employment doesn't allow you to use these preferred traits, it is important to decide whether you

Exhibit 1.1
## SELF-ASSESSMENT WORKSHEET

### Step 1. Understand Your Personal Traits

The personal traits that describe me are:
*(Include all of the words that describe you.)*
The ten personal traits that most accurately describe me are:
*(List these ten traits.)*

### Step 2. Identify Your Personal Values

Working conditions that are important to me include:
*(List working conditions that would have to exist for you to accept a position.)*
The values that go along with my working conditions are:
*(Write down the values that correspond to each working condition.)*
Some additional values I've decided to include are:
*(List those values you identify as you conduct this job search.)*

### Step 3. Calculate Your Economic Needs

My estimated minimum annual salary requirement is:
*(Write the salary you have calculated based on your budget.)*
Starting salaries for the positions I'm considering are:
*(List the name of each job you are considering and the associated starting salary.)*

### Step 4. Explore Your Longer-Term Goals

My thoughts on longer-term goals right now are:
*(Jot down some of your longer-term goals as you know them right now.)*

### Step 5. Enumerate Your Skill Base

The general skills I possess are:
*(List the skills that underlie tasks you are able to complete.)*
The specific skills I possess are:
*(List more technical or specific skills that you possess, and indicate your level of expertise.)*
General and specific skills that I want to promote to employers for the jobs I'm considering are:
*(List general and specific skills for each type of job you are considering.)*

*continued*

---

**Step 6. Recognize Your Preferred Skills**

Skills that I would like to use on the job include:

(List skills that you hope to use on the job, and indicate how often you'd like to use them.)

**Step 7. Assess Skills Needing Further Development**

Some skills that I'll need to acquire for the jobs I'm considering include:

(Write down skills listed in job advertisements or job descriptions that you don't currently possess.)

I believe I can build these skills by:

(Describe how you plan to acquire these skills.)

---

can find other ways to express them or whether you would be better off not considering this type of job. Interests and hobbies pursued outside of work hours can be one way to use personal traits you don't have an opportunity to draw on in your work. For example, if you consider yourself an outgoing person and the kinds of jobs you are examining allow little contact with other people, you may be able to achieve the level of interaction that is comfortable for you outside of your work setting. If such a compromise seems impractical or otherwise unsatisfactory, you probably should explore only jobs that provide the interaction you want and need on the job.

Many young adults who are not very confident about their employability will downplay their need for income. They will say, "Money is not all that important if I love my work." But if you begin to document exactly what you need for housing, transportation, insurance, clothing, food, and utilities, you will begin to understand that some jobs cannot meet your financial needs and it doesn't matter how wonderful the job is. If you have to worry each payday about bills and other financial obligations, you won't be very effective on the job. Begin now to be honest with yourself about your needs.

Begin the self-assessment process by creating an inventory of your personal traits. Make a list of as many words as possible to describe yourself. Words like *accurate, creative, future-oriented, relaxed,* or *structured* are just a few examples. In addition, you might ask people who know you well how they might describe you.

***Focus on Selected Personal Traits.*** Of all the traits you identified, select the ten you believe most accurately describe you. Keep track of these ten traits.

*Consider Your Personal Traits in the Job Search Process.* As you begin exploring jobs and careers, watch for matches between your personal traits and the job descriptions you read. Some jobs will require many personal traits you know you possess, and others will not seem to match those traits.

---

Working as a high school biology teacher, for example, will require many personal traits beyond your knowledge of the subject area. A teacher must be able to communicate, to motivate students, and to inspire confidence, and therefore should be outgoing, fair-minded, and imaginative. These outward traits would be more important to a teacher than to a research scientist, for example. Although both the teacher and the researcher might share an equal love of the subject matter, the personal qualities they need to function in their professions differ greatly. Researchers often work autonomously, so more inner-directed traits such as accuracy, analytical thinking, and self-motivation would be beneficial.

---

Your ability to respond to changing conditions, your decision-making ability, productivity, creativity, and verbal skills all have a bearing on your success in and enjoyment of your work life. To better guarantee success, be sure to take the time needed to understand these traits in yourself.

## Step 2   Identify Your Personal Values

Your personal values affect every aspect of your life, including employment, and they develop and change as you move through life. Values can be defined as principles that we hold in high regard, qualities that are important and desirable to us. Some values aren't ordinarily connected to work (love, beauty, color, light, relationships, family, or religion), and others are (autonomy, cooperation, effectiveness, achievement, knowledge, and security). Our values determine, in part, the level of satisfaction we feel in a particular job.

*Define Acceptable Working Conditions.* One facet of employment is the set of working conditions that must exist for someone to consider taking a job.

Each of us would probably create a unique list of acceptable working conditions, but items that might be included on many people's lists are the amount of money you would need to be paid, how far you are willing to drive or travel, the amount of freedom you want in determining your own schedule, whether you would be working with people or data or things, and the types of tasks you would be willing to do. Your conditions might include statements of working conditions you will *not* accept; for example, you might not be willing to work at night or on weekends or holidays.

If you were offered a job tomorrow, what conditions would have to exist for you to realistically consider accepting the position? Take some time and make a list of these conditions.

**Realize Associated Values.** Your list of working conditions can be used to create an inventory of your values relating to jobs and careers you are exploring. For example, if one of your conditions stated that you wanted to earn at least $30,000 per year, the associated value would be financial gain. If another condition was that you wanted to work with a friendly group of people, the value that went along with that might be belonging or interaction with people.

**Relate Your Values to the World of Work.** As you read the job descriptions you come across either in this book, in newspapers and magazines, or online, think about the values associated with each position.

---

For example, in pharmaceutical sales, your duties may include calling on clients, explaining products you offer, arranging delivery, and providing follow-up services after the sale. Associated qualities include communication, organization, and specialized knowledge.

---

At least some of the associated values in the field you're exploring should match those you extracted from your list of working conditions. Take a second look at any values that don't match up. How important are they to you? What will happen if they are not satisfied on the job? Can you incorporate those personal values elsewhere? Your answers need to be brutally honest. As you continue your exploration, be sure to add to your list any additional values that occur to you.

## Step 3   Calculate Your Economic Needs
Each of us grew up in an environment that provided for certain basic needs, such as food and shelter, and, to varying degrees, other needs that we now consider basic, such as cable television, E-mail, or an automobile. Needs such

as privacy, space, and quiet, which at first glance may not appear to be monetary needs, may add to housing expenses and so should be considered as you examine your economic needs. For example, if you place a high value on a large, open living space for yourself, it would be difficult to satisfy that need without an associated high housing cost, especially in a densely populated city environment.

As you prepare to move into the world of work and become responsible for meeting your own basic needs, it is important to consider the salary you will need to be able to afford a satisfying standard of living. The three-step process outlined here will help you plan a budget, which in turn will allow you to evaluate the various career choices and geographic locations you are considering. The steps include (1) developing a realistic budget, (2) examining starting salaries, and (3) using a cost-of-living index.

**Develop a Realistic Budget.** Each of us has certain expectations for the kind of lifestyle we want to maintain. To begin the process of defining your economic needs, it will be helpful to determine what you expect to spend on routine monthly expenses. These expenses include housing, food, transportation, entertainment, utilities, loan repayments, and revolving charge accounts. You may not currently spend anything for certain items, but you probably will have to once you begin supporting yourself. As you develop this budget, be generous in your estimates, but keep in mind any items that could be reduced or eliminated. If you are not sure about the cost of a certain item, talk with family or friends who would be able to give you a realistic estimate.

If this is new or difficult for you, start to keep a log of expenses right now. You may be surprised at how much you actually spend each month for food or stamps or magazines. Household expenses and personal grooming items can often loom very large in a budget, as can auto repairs or home maintenance.

Income taxes must also be taken into consideration when examining salary requirements. State and local taxes vary, so it is difficult to calculate exactly the effect of taxes on the amount of income you need to generate. To roughly estimate the gross income necessary to generate your minimum annual salary requirement, multiply the minimum salary you have calculated by a factor of 1.35. The resulting figure will be an approximation of what your gross income would need to be, given your estimated expenses.

**Examine Starting Salaries.** Starting salaries for each of the career tracks are provided throughout this book. These salary figures can be used in conjunction with the cost-of-living index (discussed in the next section) to determine whether you would be able to meet your basic economic needs in a given geographic location.

**Use a Cost-of-Living Index.** If you are thinking about trying to get a job in a geographic region other than the one where you now live, understanding differences in the cost of living will help you come to a more informed decision about making a move. By using a cost-of-living index, you can compare salaries offered and the cost of living in different locations with what you know about the salaries offered and the cost of living in your present location.

Many variables are used to calculate the cost-of-living index. Often included are housing, groceries, utilities, transportation, health care, clothing, and entertainment expenses. Right now you do not need to worry about the details associated with calculating a given index. The main purpose of this exercise is to help you understand that pay ranges for entry-level positions may not vary greatly, but the cost of living in different locations *can* vary tremendously.

> If you lived in Denver, Colorado, for example, and you were interested in working as a biological technician, you would earn, on average, $29,409 annually. But let's say you're also thinking about moving to New York, Los Angeles, or Cleveland. You know you can live on $29,409 in Denver, but you want to be able to equate that salary in other locations you're considering. How much will you need to earn in those locations to do this? Figuring the cost of living for each city will show you.
>
> Let's walk through this example. In any cost-of-living index, the number 100 represents the national average cost of living, and each city is assigned an index number based on current prices in that city for the items included in the index (housing, food, etc.). In the index we used here, New York was assigned the number 178, Los Angeles's index was 136, Denver's and Cleveland's indexes were both 117. In other words, it costs considerably more to live in New York than it does in Cleveland. You can set up a table to determine exactly how much you would have to earn in each of these cities to have the same buying power that you have in Denver.

## JOB: BIOLOGICAL TECHNICIAN

| City | Index | Equivalent Salary |
|------|-------|-------------------|
| New York | 178 | |
| Denver | 117 | |

$$\frac{178}{117} \times \$29,409 = \$44,742 \text{ in New York}$$

| Los Angeles | 136 | |
| Denver | 117 | |

$$\frac{136}{117} \times \$29,409 = \$34,185 \text{ in Los Angeles}$$

| Cleveland | 117 | |
| Denver | 117 | |

$$\frac{117}{117} \times \$29,409 = \$29,409 \text{ in Cleveland}$$

You would have to earn $44,742 in New York and $34,185 in Los Angeles to match the buying power of $29,409 in Denver. You could, however, live in Cleveland for the same $29,409 as in Denver.

If you would like to determine whether it's financially worthwhile to make any of these moves, one more piece of information is needed: the salaries of biological technicians in these other cities. *The American Salaries and Wages Survey* (4th edition) reports the following average salary information for biological technicians:

| Region | Annual Salary | Salary Equivalent to Denver | Change in Buying Power |
|--------|---------------|-----------------------------|------------------------|
| Mid-Atlantic (including New York) | $32,943 | $44,742 | −$11,799 |
| West (including Los Angeles) | $30,552 | $34,185 | −$3,633 |
| Midwest (including Cleveland) | $37,203 | $29,409 | +$7,794 |
| Mountain Plains (including Denver) | $29,409 | — | — |

> If you moved to New York City and secured employment as a biological technician, you would not be able to maintain the same lifestyle you led in Denver since you would need to increase your income by almost one-third to have the same lifestyle in New York. A move to Los Angeles would also decrease your buying power, though not as dramatically as a move to New York. A move to Cleveland, however, would considerably increase your buying power given the rate of pay and cost of living there.

You can work through a similar exercise for any type of job you are considering and for many locations when current salary information is available. It will be worth your time to undertake this analysis if you are seriously considering a relocation. By doing so you will be able to make an informed choice.

## Step 4   Explore Your Longer-Term Goals

There is no question that when we first begin working, our goals are to use our skills and education in a job that will reward us with employment, income, and status relative to the preparation we brought with us to this position. If we are not being paid as much as we feel we should for our level of education or if job demands don't provide the intellectual stimulation we had hoped for, we experience unhappiness and as a result often seek other employment.

Most jobs we consider "good" are those that fulfill our basic "lower-level" needs of security, food, clothing, shelter, income, and productive work. But even when our basic needs are met and our jobs are secure and productive, we as individuals are constantly changing. As we change, the demands and expectations we place on our jobs may change. Fortunately, some jobs grow and change with us, and this explains why some people are happy throughout many years in a job.

But more often people are bigger than the jobs they fill. We have more goals and needs than any job could satisfy. These are "higher-level" needs of self-esteem, companionship, affection, and an increasing desire to feel we are employing ourselves in the most effective way possible. Not all of these higher-level needs can be met through employment, but for as long as we are employed, we increasingly demand that our jobs play their part in moving us along the path to fulfillment.

Another obvious but important fact is that we change as we mature. Although our jobs also have the potential for change, they may not change as frequently or as markedly as we do. There are increasingly fewer one-job, one-employer careers; we must think about a work future that may involve voluntary or forced moves from employer to employer. Because of that very real possibility, we need to take advantage of the opportunities in each position we hold. Acquiring the skills and competencies associated with each position will keep us viable and attractive as employees. This is particularly true in a job market that not only is technology/computer dependent, but also is populated with more and more small, self-transforming organizations rather than the large, seemingly stable organizations of the past.

---

For example, if you are interested in a career as an animal curator in a zoo, it would be helpful to talk with an entry-level animal caretaker, then a more experienced assistant zookeeper, and finally an animal department supervisor or experienced curator. Each of these people will be able to offer a different perspective on the field, providing insight into any unique concerns and helping you determine whether you are pursuing the best path for your future.

---

## Step 5   Enumerate Your Skill Base

In terms of the job search, skills can be thought of as capabilities that can be developed in school, at work, or by volunteering and then used in specific job settings. Many studies have documented the kinds of skills that employers seek in entry-level applicants. For example, some of the most desired skills for individuals interested in the teaching profession are the ability to interact effectively with students one-on-one, to manage a classroom, to adapt to varying situations as necessary, and to get involved in school activities. Business employers have also identified important qualities, including enthusiasm for the employer's product or service, a businesslike mind, the ability to follow written or oral instructions, the ability to demonstrate self-control, the confidence to suggest new ideas, the ability to communicate with all members of a group, an awareness of cultural differences, and loyalty, to name just a few. You will find that many of these skills are also in the repertoire of qualities demanded in your college major.

To be successful in obtaining any given job, you must be able to demonstrate that you possess a certain mix of skills that will allow you to carry out the duties required by that job. This skill mix will vary a great deal from job to job; to determine the skills necessary for the jobs you are seeking, you can read job advertisements or more generic job descriptions, such as those found later in this book. If you want to be effective in the job search, you must directly show employers that you possess the skills needed to be successful in filling the position. These skills will initially be described on your résumé and then discussed again during the interview process.

Skills are either general or specific. To develop a list of skills relevant to employers, you must first identify the general skills you possess, then list specific skills you have to offer, and, finally, examine which of these skills employers are seeking.

***Identify Your General Skills.*** Because you possess or will possess a college degree, employers will assume that you can read and write, perform certain basic computations, think critically, and communicate effectively. Employers will want to see that you have acquired these skills, and they will want to know which additional general skills you possess.

One way to begin identifying skills is to write an experiential diary. An experiential diary lists all the tasks you were responsible for completing for each job you've held and then outlines the skills required to do those tasks. You may list several skills for any given task. This diary allows you to distinguish between the tasks you performed and the underlying skills required to complete those tasks. Here's an example:

| Tasks | Skills |
|---|---|
| Answering telephone | Effective use of language, clear diction, ability to direct inquiries, ability to solve problems |
| Waiting on tables | Poise under conditions of time and pressure, speed, accuracy, good memory, simultaneous completion of tasks, sales skills |

For each job or experience you have participated in, develop a worksheet based on the example shown here. On a résumé, you may want to describe these skills rather than simply listing tasks. Skills are easier for the employer to appreciate, especially when your experience is very different from the employment you are seeking. In addition to helping you identify general skills, this experiential diary will prepare you to speak more effectively in an interview about the qualifications you possess.

***Identify Your Specific Skills.*** It may be easier to identify your specific skills because you can definitely say whether you can speak other languages, program a computer, draft a map or diagram, or edit a document using appropriate symbols and terminology.

Using your experiential diary, identify the points in your history where you learned how to do something very specific, and decide whether you have a beginning, intermediate, or advanced knowledge of how to use that particular skill. Right now, be sure to list *every* specific skill you have, and don't consider whether you like using the skill. Write down a list of specific skills you have acquired and the level of competence you possess—beginning, intermediate, or advanced.

***Relate Your Skills to Employers.*** You probably have thought about a couple of different jobs you might be interested in obtaining, and one way to begin relating the general and specific skills you possess to a potential employer's needs is to read actual advertisements for these types of positions (see Part Two for resources listing actual job openings).

---

For example, you might be interested in a career as an animal behaviorist. A typical job listing might read, "Requires 3 to 5 years of experience, organizational and interpersonal skills, imagination, drive, and the ability to work under pressure." If you then used any one of a number of general sources of information that describe the job of an animal behaviorist, you would find additional information. Depending on the setting in which they work, animal behaviorists also develop training programs, methods, and schedules; teach animal trainers; advise and consult with animal handlers; conduct research; provide information to the public; and possess thorough knowledge about the animal world.

Begin by building a comprehensive list of required skills with the first job description you read. Exploring advertisements for and descriptions of several types of related positions will reveal an important core of skills necessary for obtaining the type of work you're interested in. In building this list, include both general and specific skills.

On a separate sheet of paper, try to generate a comprehensive list of required skills for at least one job you are considering. The list of general skills that you develop for a given career path would be valuable for any number of jobs you might apply for. Many of the specific skills would also be transferable to other types of positions. For example, the ability to solve problems would be a necessary skill for animal behaviorists, and it would also be important for curators working in a zoo.

Following is a sample list of skills needed to be successful as an animal behaviorist. These items were extracted from general resources and actual job listings.

## JOB: ANIMAL BEHAVIORIST

| General Skills | Specific Skills |
|---|---|
| Disseminate information | Write articles, books, manuals |
| Have a specific body of knowledge | Speak publicly |
| Gather information | Write letters and memos |
| Writing | Write grants |
| Work well with people | Propose projects |
| Work well with animals | Conduct research |
| Exhibit creativity | Analyze research data |
| Observation skills | Present exhibitions |
| Analytical thinking | Demonstrate techniques |
| Problem solving | Develop specific training |
| Evaluation skills | methods |

Now review the list of skills you developed and check off those skills that *you know you possess* and that are required for jobs you are considering. You should refer to these specific skills on the résumé that you write for this type of job. See Chapter 2 for details on résumé writing.

## Step 6 Recognize Your Preferred Skills

In the previous section you developed a comprehensive list of skills that relate to particular career paths that are of interest to you. You can now relate these to skills that you prefer to use. We all use a wide range of skills (some researchers say individuals have a repertoire of about five hundred skills), but we may not particularly be interested in using all of them in our work. There may be some skills that come to us more naturally or that we use successfully time and time again and that we want to continue to use; these are best described as our preferred skills. For this exercise use the list of skills that you created for the previous section, and decide which of them you are *most interested in using* in future work and how often you would like to use them. You might be interested in using some skills only occasionally, while others you would like to use more regularly. You probably also have skills that you hope you can use constantly.

As you examine job announcements, look for matches between this list of preferred skills and the qualifications described in the advertisements. These skills should be highlighted on your résumé and discussed in job interviews.

## Step 7    Assess Skills Needing Further Development

Previously you compiled a list of general and specific skills required for given positions. You already possess some of these skills; those that remain to be developed are your underdeveloped skills.

If you are just beginning the job search, there may be gaps between the qualifications required for some of the jobs you're considering and the skills you possess. The thought of having to admit to and talk about these underdeveloped skills, especially in a job interview, is a frightening one. One way to put a healthy perspective on this subject is to target and relate your exploration of underdeveloped skills to the types of positions you are seeking. Recognizing these shortcomings and planning to overcome them with either on-the-job training or additional formal education can be a positive way to address the concept of underdeveloped skills.

On your worksheet or in your journal, make a list of up to five general or specific skills required for the positions you're interested in that you *don't currently possess*. For each item list an idea you have for specific action you could take to acquire that skill. Do some brainstorming to come up with possible actions. If you have a hard time generating ideas, talk to people currently working in this type of position, professionals in your college career services office, trusted friends, family members, or members of related professional associations.

In the chapter on interviewing, we will discuss in detail how to effectively address questions about underdeveloped skills. Generally speaking, though, employers want genuine answers to these types of questions. They want you to reveal "the real you," and they also want to see how you answer difficult questions. In taking the positive, targeted approach discussed previously, you show the employer that you are willing to continue to learn and that you have a plan for strengthening your job qualifications.

## Use Your Self-Assessment

Exploring entry-level career options can be an exciting experience if you have good resources available and will take the time to use them. Can you effectively complete the following tasks?

1. Understand your personality traits and relate them to career choices
2. Define your personal values
3. Determine your economic needs
4. Explore longer-term goals
5. Understand your skill base
6. Recognize your preferred skills
7. Express a willingness to improve on your underdeveloped skills

If so, then you can more meaningfully participate in the job search process by writing a more effective résumé, finding job titles that represent work you are interested in doing, locating job sites that will provide the opportunity for you to use your strengths and skills, networking in an informed way, participating in focused interviews, getting the most out of follow-up contacts, and evaluating job offers to find those that create a good match between you and the employer. The remaining chapters in Part One guide you through these next steps in the job search process. For many job seekers, this process can take anywhere from three months to a year to implement. The time you will need to put into your job search will depend on the type of job you want and the geographic location where you'd like to work. Think of your effort as a job in itself, requiring you to set aside time each week to complete the needed work. Carefully undertaken efforts may reduce the time you need for your job search.

# 2

# The Résumé and Cover Letter

The task of writing a résumé may seem overwhelming if you are unfamiliar with this type of document, but there are some easily understood techniques that can and should be used. This section was written to help you understand the purpose of the résumé, the different types of résumé formats available, and how to write the sections of information traditionally found on a résumé. We will present examples and explanations that address questions frequently posed by people writing their first résumé or updating an old résumé.

Even within the formats and suggestions given, however, there are infinite variations. True, most résumés follow one of the outlines suggested, but you should feel free to adjust the résumé to suit your needs and make it expressive of your life and experience.

## Why Write a Résumé?

The purpose of a résumé is to convince an employer that you should be interviewed. Whether you're mailing, faxing, or E-mailing this document, you'll want to present enough information to show that you can make an immediate and valuable contribution to an organization. A résumé is not an in-depth historical or legal document; later in the job search process you may be asked to document your entire work history on an application form and attest to its validity. The résumé should, instead, highlight relevant information pertaining directly to the organization that will receive the document or to the type of position you are seeking.

We will discuss the chronological and digital résumés in detail here. Functional and targeted résumés, which are used much less often, are briefly discussed. The reasons for using one type of résumé over another and the typical format for each are addressed in the following sections.

# The Chronological Résumé

The chronological résumé is the most common of the various résumé formats and therefore the format that employers are most used to receiving. This type of résumé is easy to read and understand because it details the chronological progression of jobs you have held. (See Exhibit 2.1.) It begins with your most recent employment and works back in time. If you have a solid work history or have experience that provided growth and development in your duties and responsibilities, a chronological résumé will highlight these achievements. The typical elements of a chronological résumé include the heading, a career objective, educational background, employment experience, activities, and references.

### The Heading
The heading consists of your name, address, telephone number, and other means of contact. This may include a fax number, E-mail address, and your home-page address. If you are using a shared E-mail account or a parent's business fax, be sure to let others who use these systems know that you may receive important professional correspondence via these systems. You wouldn't want to miss a vital E-mail or fax! Likewise, if your résumé directs readers to a personal home page on the Web, be certain it's a professional personal home page designed to be viewed and appreciated by a prospective employer. This may mean making substantial changes in the home page you currently mount on the Web.

### The Objective
Without a doubt the objective statement is the most challenging part of the résumé for most writers. Even for individuals who have decided on a career path, it can be difficult to encapsulate all they want to say in one or two brief sentences. For job seekers who are unfocused or unclear about their intentions, trying to write this section can inhibit the entire résumé writing process.

Keep the objective as short as possible and no longer than two short sentences.

Exhibit 2.1
## CHRONOLOGICAL RÉSUMÉ

### REESE CONNORS

188 Beacon Street #12
Boston, MA 02125
(617) 555-3455
r_connors@xxx.com

### OBJECTIVE
A position as an aquarist or trainer at an aquarium in California, working with marine mammals.

### EDUCATION
Bachelor of Science Degree in Biology
Salem State College, Salem, Massachusetts, May 2003
Concentration: Marine Biology
Minor: Chemistry
Overall GPA: 3.2

### EXPERIENCE
Internship. Diving Aquarist (Junior)
187,000-gallon, Giant Ocean Tank Caribbean Coral Reef Exhibit
New England Aquarium, Boston, Massachusetts
Year-to-year internship, twenty hours a week, helping maintain the tank and participating in collecting trips.

### 2000 to Present
Internship. Aquarist-in-Training
Penguin Exhibit
New England Aquarium, Boston, Massachusetts
Nine-month program, assisting in the penguin colony, feeding the penguins, banding them, participating in presentations, and caring for the tank.

### 1999–2000
Volunteer. Junior Keeper, Petting Zoo
Franklin Park Zoo, Boston, Massachusetts

*continued*

**Summer 1999**
Volunteer position three days a week, working in the petting zoo, feeding and bathing the animals, and assisting visitors, including children and their parents. Responsible also for ensuring the safety of visitors and animals.

**ADDITIONAL QUALIFICATIONS**
Advanced PADI SCUBA Diving Certificate

**REFERENCES**
Available upon request.

Choose one of the following types of objective statement:

## 1. General Objective Statement

- An entry-level educational programming coordinator position

## 2. Position-Focused Objective

- To obtain the position of conference coordinator at State College

## 3. Industry-Focused Objective

- To begin a career as a sales representative in the cruise line industry

## 4. Summary of Qualifications Statement

A degree in biology and four years of progressively increasing responsibilities in the curatorial department of a major aquarium have prepared me for a career as assistant curator in an institution that values hands-on involvement and thoroughness.

**Support Your Objective.** A résumé that contains any one of these types of objective statements should then go on to demonstrate why you are qualified to get the position. Listing academic degrees can be one way to indicate qualifications. Another demonstration would be in the way previous experiences, both volunteer and paid, are described. Without this kind of documentation in the body of the résumé, the objective looks unsupported. Think of the résumé as telling a connected story about you. All the elements should work together to form a coherent picture that ideally should relate to your statement of objective.

## Education

This section of your résumé should indicate the exact name of the degree you will receive or have received, spelled out completely with no abbreviations. The degree is generally listed after the objective, followed by the institution name and location, and then the month and year of graduation. This section could also include your academic minor, grade point average (GPA), and appearance on the Dean's List or President's List.

If you have enough space, you might want to include a section listing courses related to the field in which you are seeking work. The best use of a "related courses" section would be to list some course work that is not traditionally associated with the major. Perhaps you took several computer courses outside your degree that will be helpful and related to the job prospects you are entertaining. Several education section examples are shown here:

- Bachelor of Science Degree in Biology
  University of Florida, Gainesville, Florida, June 2004
  Concentration: Botany
- Bachelor of Science Degree in Biology
  Tufts University, Medford, Massachusetts, May 2004
  Minor: Marine Biology
- Bachelor of Arts Degree in Secondary Education
  University of New Mexico, Albuquerque, New Mexico,
  June 2004
  Concentration: Biology

An example of a format for a related-courses section follows:

| RELATED COURSES | |
| --- | --- |
| Chemistry | Psychology |
| Taxonomy | Ecology |
| Oceanography | Research Methods |

## Experience

The experience section of your résumé should be the most substantial part and should take up most of the space on the page. Employers want to see what kind of work history you have. They will look at your range of experiences, longevity in jobs, and specific tasks you are able to complete. This section may also be called "work experience," "related experience," "employment history," or "employment." No matter what you call this section, some important points to remember are the following:

1. **Describe your duties** as they relate to the position you are seeking.
2. **Emphasize major responsibilities** and indicate increases in responsibility. Include all relevant employment experiences: summer, part-time, internships, cooperative education, or self-employment.
3. **Emphasize skills**, especially those that transfer from one situation to another. The fact that you coordinated a student organization, chaired meetings, supervised others, and managed a budget leads one to suspect that you could coordinate other things as well.
4. **Use descriptive job titles** that provide information about what you did. A "Student Intern" should be more specifically stated as, for example, "Magazine Operations Intern." "Volunteer" is also too general; a title such as "Peer Writing Tutor" would be more appropriate.
5. **Create word pictures** by using active verbs to start sentences. Describe *results* you have produced in the work you have done.

A limp description would say something such as the following: "My duties included helping with production, proofreading, and editing. I used a design and page layout program." An action statement would be stated as follows: "Coordinated and assisted in the creative marketing of brochures and seminar promotions, becoming proficient in Quark."

Remember, an accomplishment is simply a result, a final measurable product that people can relate to. A duty is not a result; it is an obligation—every job holder has duties. For an effective résumé, list as many results as you can. To make the most of the limited space you have and to give your description impact, carefully select appropriate and accurate descriptors.

Here are some traits that employers tell us they like to see:

• Teamwork
• Energy and motivation

- Learning and using new skills
- Versatility
- Critical thinking
- Understanding how profits are created
- Organizational acumen
- Communicating directly and clearly, in both writing and speaking
- Risk taking
- Willingness to admit mistakes
- High personal standards

## Solutions to Frequently Encountered Problems

### Repetitive Employment with the Same Employer
EMPLOYMENT: The Foot Locker, Portland, Oregon. Summer 2001, 2002, 2003. Initially employed in high school as salesclerk. Due to successful performance, asked to return next two summers at higher pay with added responsibility. Ranked as the #2 salesperson the first summer and #1 the next two summers. Assisted in arranging eye-catching retail displays; served as manager of other summer workers during owner's absence.

### A Large Number of Jobs
EMPLOYMENT: Recent Hospitality Industry Experience: Affiliated with four upscale hotel/restaurant complexes (September 2001–February 2004), where I worked part- and full-time as a waiter, bartender, disc jockey, and bookkeeper to produce income for college.

### Several Positions with the Same Employer
EMPLOYMENT: Coca-Cola Bottling Co., Burlington, Vermont, 2001–2004. In four years, I received three promotions, each with increased pay and responsibility.

*Summer Sales Coordinator:* Promoted to hire, train, and direct efforts of add-on staff of fifteen college-age route salespeople hired to meet summer peak demand for product.

*Sales Administrator:* Promoted to run home office sales desk, managing accounts and associated delivery schedules for professional sales force of ten people. Intensive phone work, daily interaction with all personnel, and strong knowledge of product line required.

*Route Salesperson:* Summer employment to travel and tourism industry sites that use Coke products. Met specific schedule demands, used good communication skills with wide variety of customers, and demonstrated strong selling skills. Named salesperson of the month for July and August of that year.

## Questions Résumé Writers Often Ask

### How Far Back Should I Go in Terms of Listing Past Jobs?

Usually, listing three or four jobs should suffice. If you did something back in high school that has a bearing on your future aspirations for employment, by all means list the job. As you progress through your college career, high school jobs will be replaced on the résumé by college employment.

### Should I Differentiate Between Paid and Nonpaid Employment?

Most employers are not initially concerned about how much you were paid. They are anxious to know how much responsibility you held in your past employment. There is no need to specify that your work was as a volunteer if you had significant responsibilities.

### How Should I Represent My Accomplishments or Work-Related Responsibilities?

Succinctly, but fully. In other words, give the employer enough information to arouse curiosity but not so much detail that you leave nothing to the imagination. Besides, some jobs merit more lengthy explanations than others. Be sure to convey any information that can give an employer a better understanding of the depth of your involvement at work. Did you supervise others? How many? Did your efforts result in a more efficient operation? How much did you increase efficiency? Did you handle a budget? How much? Were you promoted in a short time? Did you work two jobs at once or fifteen hours per week after high school? Where appropriate, quantify.

### Should the Work Section Always Follow the Education Section on the Résumé?

Always lead with your strengths. If your education closely relates to the employment you now seek, put this section after the objective. If your education does not closely relate but you have a surplus of good work experiences, consider reversing the order of your sections to lead with employment, followed by education.

### How Should I Present My Activities, Honors, Awards, Professional Societies, and Affiliations?

This section of the résumé can add valuable information for an employer to consider if used correctly. The rule of thumb for information in this section is to include only those activities that are in some way relevant to the objective stated on your résumé. If you can draw a valid connection between your activities and your objective, include them; if not, leave them out.

Professional affiliations and honors should all be listed; especially important are those related to your job objective. Social clubs and activities need not be a part of your résumé unless you hold a significant office or you are looking for a position related to your membership. Be aware that most prospective employers' principal concerns are related to your employability, not your social life. If you have any, publications can be included as an addendum to your résumé.

### How Should I Handle References?

The use of references is considered a part of the interview process, and they should never be listed on a résumé. You would always provide references to a potential employer if requested to, so it is not even necessary to include this section on the résumé if space does not permit. If space is available, it is acceptable to include the following statement:

- REFERENCES: Furnished upon request.

## The Functional Résumé

The functional résumé departs from a chronological résumé in that it organizes information by specific accomplishments in various settings: previous jobs, volunteer work, associations, and so forth. This type of résumé permits you to stress the substance of your experiences rather than the position titles you have held. You should consider using a functional résumé if you have held a series of similar jobs that relied on the same skills or abilities. There are many good books in which you can find examples of functional résumés, including *How to Write a Winning Resume* or *Resumes Made Easy.*

# The Targeted Résumé

The targeted résumé focuses on specific work-related capabilities you can bring to a given position within an organization. Past achievements are listed to highlight your capabilities and the work history section is abbreviated.

# Digital Résumés

Today's employers have to manage an enormous number of résumés. One of the most frequent complaints the writers of this series hear from students is the failure of employers to even acknowledge the receipt of a résumé and cover letter. Frequently, the reason for this poor response or nonresponse is the volume of applications received for every job. In an attempt to better manage the considerable labor investment involved in processing large numbers of résumés, many employers are requiring digital submission of résumés. There are two types of digital résumés: those that can be E-mailed or posted to a website, called *electronic résumés*, and those that can be "read" by a computer, commonly called *scannable résumés*. Though the format may be a bit different from the traditional "paper" résumé, the goal of both types of digital résumés is the same—to get you an interview! These résumés must be designed to be "technologically friendly." What that basically means to you is that they should be free of graphics and fancy formatting. (See Exhibit 2.2.)

## Electronic Résumés

Sometimes referred to as plain-text résumés, electronic résumés are designed to be E-mailed to an employer or posted to one of many commercial Internet databases such as CareerMosaic.com, America's Job Bank (ajb.dni.us), or Monster.com.

Some technical considerations:

- Electronic résumés must be written in American Standard Code for Information Interchange (ASCII), which is simply a plain-text format. These characters are universally recognized so that every computer can accurately read and understand them. To create an ASCII file of your current résumé, open your document, then save it as a text or ASCII file. This will eliminate all formatting. Edit as needed using your computer's text editor application.
- Use a standard-width typeface. Courier is a good choice because it is the font associated with ASCII in most systems.

Exhibit 2.2
## DIGITAL RÉSUMÉ

REESE CONNORS ◄──────────────────── Put your name at the
188 Beacon Street #12                              top on its own line.
Boston, MA 02125
Phone: 617-555-3455 ◄────────────
r_connors@xxx.com ──────────────── Put your phone number
                                                          on its own line.

KEYWORD SUMMARY ◄────────────
Bachelor's in Marine Biology                    Keywords make your
Aquarist                                                   résumé easier to find in
SCUBA                                                      a database.

                                                          Use a standard-width
WORK EXPERIENCE                                 typeface.
New England Aquarium, Boston, Massachusetts
Intern, Diving Aquarist (Junior)
2002 to Present ────────────────── Use a space between
* Year-to-year internship, twenty hours a week,  asterisk and text.
helping maintain the coral reef tank and participating
in collecting trips.                                No line should exceed
                                                          sixty-five characters.

New England Aquarium, Boston, Massachusetts
Intern, Aquarist-in-Training
1999-2000
* Nine-month program, assisting in the penguin
colony, feeding the penguins, banding them,
participating in presentations, and caring for the tank.

                                                          End each line by
Franklin Park Zoo, Boston, Massachusetts        hitting the ENTER
Volunteer, Junior Keeper, Petting Zoo           (or RETURN) key.
Summer 1999
* Volunteer position three days a week, working in
the petting zoo, feeding and bathing the animals, and
assisting visitors, including children and their parents.
Responsible also for ensuring the safety of visitors
and animals.

*continued*

EDUCATION ◄─────────────────────────── Capitalize letters to
                                              emphasize headings.
Bachelor of Science Degree in Biology
Salem State College, Salem, Massachusetts,
May 2003
Concentration: Marine Biology
Minor: Chemistry
Overall GPA: 3.2

- Use a font size of 11 to 14 points. A 12-point font is considered standard.
- Your margin should be left-justified.
- Do not exceed sixty-five characters per line because the word-wrap function doesn't operate in ASCII.
- Do not use boldface, italics, underlining, bullets, or various font sizes. Instead, use asterisks, plus signs, or all capital letters when you want to emphasize something.
- Avoid graphics and shading.
- Use as many "keywords" as you possibly can. These are words or phrases usually relating to skills or experience that either are specifically used in the job announcement or are popular buzzwords in the industry.
- Minimize abbreviations.
- Your name should be the first line of text.
- Conduct a "test run" by E-mailing your résumé to yourself and a friend before you send it to the employer. See how it transmits, and make any changes you need to. Continue to test it until it's exactly how you want it to look.
- Unless an employer specifically requests that you send the résumé in the form of an attachment, don't. Employers can encounter problems opening a document as an attachment, and there are always viruses to consider.
- Don't forget your cover letter. Send it along with your résumé as a single message.

## Scannable Résumés

Some companies are relying on technology to narrow the candidate pool for available job openings. Electronic Applicant Tracking uses imaging to scan, sort, and store résumé elements in a database. Then, through OCR (Optical Character Recognition) software, the computer scans the résumés for keywords and phrases. To have the best chance at getting an interview, you want to increase the number of "hits"—matches of your skills, abilities, experience, and education to those the computer is scanning for—your résumé will get. You can see how critical using the right keywords is for this type of résumé.

Technical considerations include:

- Again, do not use boldface (newer systems may read this OK, but many older ones won't), italics, underlining, bullets, shading, graphics, or multiple font sizes. Instead, for emphasis, use asterisks, plus signs, or all capital letters. Minimize abbreviations.
- Use a popular typeface such as Courier, Helvetica, Ariel, or Palatino. Avoid decorative fonts.
- Font size should be between 11 and 14 points.
- Do not compress the spacing between letters.
- Use horizontal and vertical lines sparingly; the computer may misread them as the letters *L* or *I*.
- Left-justify the text.
- Do not use parentheses or brackets around telephone numbers, and be sure your phone number is on its own line of text.
- Your name should be the first line of text and on its own line. If your résumé is longer than one page, be sure to put your name on the top of all pages.
- Use a traditional résumé structure. The chronological format may work best.
- Use nouns that are skill-focused, such as *management, writer,* and *programming.* This is different from traditional paper résumés, which use action-oriented verbs.
- Laser printers produce the finest copies. Avoid dot-matrix printers.
- Use standard, light-colored paper with text on one side only. Since the higher the contrast, the better, your best choice is black ink on white paper.
- Always send original copies. If you must fax, set the fax on fine mode, not standard.
- Do not staple or fold your résumé. This can confuse the computer.
- Before you send your scannable résumé, be certain the employer uses this technology. If you can't determine this, you may want to send two versions (scannable and traditional) to be sure your résumé gets considered.

## Résumé Production and Other Tips

An ink-jet printer is the preferred option for printing your résumé. Begin by printing just a few copies. You may find a small error or you may simply want to make some changes, and it is less frustrating and less expensive if you print in small batches.

Résumé paper color should be carefully chosen. You should consider the types of employers who will receive your résumé and the types of positions for which you are applying. Use white or ivory paper for traditional or conservative employers or for higher-level positions.

Black ink on sharp, white paper can be harsh on the reader's eyes. Think about an ivory or cream paper that will provide less contrast and be easier to read. Pink, green, and blue tints should generally be avoided.

Many résumé writers buy packages of matching envelopes and cover sheet stationery that, although not absolutely necessary, help convey a professional impression.

If you'll be producing many cover letters at home, be sure you have high-quality printing equipment. Learn standard envelope formats for business, and retain a copy of every cover letter you send out. You can use the copies to take notes of any telephone conversations that may occur.

If attending a job fair, either carry a briefcase or place your résumé in a nicely covered legal-size pad holder.

## The Cover Letter

The cover letter provides you with the opportunity to tailor your résumé by telling the prospective employer how you can be a benefit to the organization. It allows you to highlight aspects of your background that are not already discussed in your résumé and that might be especially relevant to the organization you are contacting or to the position you are seeking. Every résumé should have a cover letter enclosed when you send it out. Unlike the résumé, which may be mass-produced, a cover letter is most effective when it is individually prepared and focused on the particular requirements of the organization in question.

A good cover letter should supplement the résumé and motivate the reader to review the résumé. The format shown in Exhibit 2.3 (see page 34) is only a suggestion to help you decide what information to include in a cover letter.

Begin the cover letter with your street address six lines down from the top. Leave three to five lines between the date and the name of the person to whom you are addressing the cover letter. Make sure you leave one blank line between the salutation and the body of the letter and between paragraphs. After typing "Sincerely," leave four blank lines and type your name. This should leave plenty of room for your signature. A sample cover letter is shown in Exhibit 2.4 on page 35.

The following guidelines will help you write good cover letters:

1. Be sure to type your letter neatly; ensure there are no misspellings.
2. Avoid unusual typefaces, such as script.
3. Address the letter to an individual, using the person's name and title. To obtain this information, call the company. If answering a blind newspaper advertisement, address the letter "To Whom It May Concern" or omit the salutation.
4. Be sure your cover letter directly indicates the position you are applying for and tells why you are qualified to fill it.
5. Send the original letter, not a photocopy, with your résumé. Keep a copy for your records.
6. Make your cover letter no more than one page.
7. Include a phone number where you can be reached.
8. Avoid trite language and have someone read the letter over to react to its tone, content, and mechanics.
9. For your own information, record the date you send out each letter and résumé.

Exhibit 2.3
## COVER LETTER FORMAT

Your Street Address
Your Town, State, Zip
Phone Number
Fax Number
E-mail

Date

Name
Title
Organization
Address

Dear _____:

*First Paragraph.* In this paragraph state the reason for the letter, name the specific position or type of work you are applying for, and indicate from which resource (career services office, website, newspaper, contact, employment service) you learned of this opening. The first paragraph can also be used to inquire about future openings.

*Second Paragraph.* Indicate why you are interested in this position, the company, or its products or services, and what you can do for the employer. If you are a recent graduate, explain how your academic background makes you a qualified candidate. Try not to repeat the same information found in the résumé.

*Third Paragraph.* Refer the reader to the enclosed résumé for more detailed information.

*Fourth Paragraph.* In this paragraph say what you will do to follow up on your letter. For example, state that you will call by a certain date to set up an interview or to find out if the company will be recruiting in your area. Finish by indicating your willingness to answer any questions the recipient may have. Be sure you have provided your phone number.

Sincerely,

*Type your name*
Enclosure

Exhibit 2.4
## SAMPLE COVER LETTER

Richard Stern
435 NE 45 Court
Fort Lauderdale, FL 33309
(954) 555-2213
sternrichard@xxx.com

April 25, 2004

Peter Schreiber
Director of Personnel
Sea World
P.O. Box 555
Orlando, FL 31455

Dear Mr. Schreiber:

In May of 2004 I will graduate from the University of Miami with a bachelor of science degree in biology. I read of your opening for an assistant trainer experienced with marine mammals in the Sunday, April 24 *Orlando Sentinel*. I am very interested in the possibilities the position offers and would like to explore the opportunity for employment at Sea World.

The ad indicated that you are looking for hard-working individuals with good communication skills, who also have experience in training, medical, show, and research behaviors. I believe that I possess all of these skills. During summers while in college I worked at the Miami Seaquarium in several capacities, including an internship working with sea lions and a stint as an aquarist-in-training, maintaining the tank. Through my work there, I learned the importance of possessing good observation skills and maintaining a positive attitude with coworkers and visitors.

In addition to the various animal behavior courses in my academic program, I felt it important to enroll in some history, anthropology, and psychology courses, focusing particularly on training module design and methods. These courses helped me become comfortable with understanding marine mammals and honed my research skills. I believe these accomplishments will enable me to

*continued*

represent Sea World in a professional and enthusiastic manner. The enclosed résumé provides a complete summary of my experience and qualifications.

I would like to meet with you to discuss how my education and experience meet your needs. I will contact your office next week to discuss the possibility of an interview. In the meantime, if you have any questions or require additional information, please contact me at (954) 555-2213 or sternrichard@xxx.com.

Sincerely,

Richard Stern
Enclosure

# 3

# Researching Careers and Networking

---

"What can I do with my degree?" is a question heard frequently by career counselors. Biology majors have many options, but a good number of them are not immediately obvious. Many biology graduates face this problem, because unlike students in narrowly defined disciplines such as accounting, computer science, or the performing arts, they do not have an automatic career path to pursue. While graduates in accounting and computer science usually know what types of jobs they will seek, just what sort of work can biology majors look for?

---

## What Do They Call the Job You Want?

One reason for confusion is perhaps a mistaken assumption that a college education provides job training. In most cases it does not. Of course, applied fields such as engineering, management, or education provide specific skills for the workplace as well as an education. Regardless, your overall college education exposes you to numerous fields of study and teaches you quantitative reasoning, critical thinking, writing, and speaking, all of which can be successfully applied to a number of different job fields. But it still remains up to you to choose a job field and to learn how to articulate the benefits of your education in a way the employer will appreciate.

### Collect Job Titles
The world of employment is a complex place, so you need to become a bit of an explorer and adventurer and be willing to try a variety of techniques

to develop a list of possible occupations that might use your talents and education. You might find computerized interest inventories, reference books and other sources, and classified ads helpful in this respect. Once you have a list of possibilities that you are interested in and qualified for, you can move on to find out what kinds of organizations have these job titles.

**Computerized Interest Inventories.** One way to begin collecting job titles is to identify a number of jobs that call for your degree and the particular skills and interests you identified as part of the self-assessment process. There are excellent interactive career-guidance programs on the market to help you produce such selected lists of possible job titles. Most of these are available at colleges and at some larger town and city libraries. Two of the industry leaders are *CHOICES* and *DISCOVER*. Both allow you to enter interests, values, educational background, and other information to produce lists of possible occupations and industries. Each of the resources listed here will produce different job title lists. Some job titles will appear again and again, while others will be unique to a particular source. Investigate all of them!

**Reference Sources.** Books on the market that may be available through your local library or career counseling office also suggest various occupations related to specific majors. The following are only a few of the many good books on the market: *The College Board Guide to 150 Popular College Majors, College Majors and Careers: A Resource Guide for Effective Life Planning* both by Paul Phifer, and *Kaplan's What to Study: 101 Fields in a Flash*. All of these books list possible job titles within the academic major.

---

The Occupational Outlook Handbook, or OOH, lists more than two dozen related job titles for biology majors. You will find familiar titles such as botanist and ecologist, as well as more specialized titles such as limnologist and cytologist. Biologist is a broad title, and most biologists are classified by the type of organism they study or specific activity they perform.

Occupational Projections and Training Data is another useful resource. Here you can compare five hundred occupations based on factors such as job openings, earnings, and training requirements.

Using these two resources, you might find the job title of ecologist in the OOH and then compare it with other jobs

related to that title in *Occupational Projections and Training Data.*
This will allow you to evaluate statistics in several different
jobs within the field.

---

Each job title deserves your consideration. Like removing the layers of an onion, the search for job titles can go on and on! As you spend time doing this activity, you are actually learning more about the value of your degree. What's important in your search at this point is not to become critical or selective but rather to develop as long a list of possibilities as you can. Every source used will help you add new and potentially exciting jobs to your growing list.

**Classified Ads.** It has been well publicized that the classified ad section of the newspaper represents only a small fraction of the current job market. Nevertheless, the weekly classified ads can be a great help to you in your search. Although they may not be the best place to look for a job, they can teach you a lot about the job market. Classified ads provide a good education in job descriptions, duties, responsibilities, and qualifications. In addition, they provide insight into which industries are actively recruiting and some indication of the area's employment market. This is particularly helpful when seeking a position in a specific geographic area and/or a specific field. For your purposes, classified ads are a good source for job titles to add to your list.

Read the Sunday classified ads in a major market newspaper for several weeks in a row. Cut and paste all the ads that interest you and seem to call for something close to your education, skills, experience, and interests. Remember that classified ads are written for what an organization *hopes* to find, you don't have to meet absolutely every criterion. However, if certain requirements are stated as absolute minimums and you cannot meet them, it's best not to waste your time and that of the employer.

The weekly classified want ads exercise is important because these jobs are out in the marketplace. They truly exist, and people with your qualifications are being sought to apply. What's more, many of these advertisements describe the duties and responsibilities of the job advertised and give you a beginning sense of the challenges and opportunities such a position presents. Some will indicate salary, and that will be helpful as well. This information will better define the jobs for you and provide some good material for possible interviews in that field.

## Explore Job Descriptions

Once you've arrived at a solid list of possible job titles that interest you and for which you believe you are somewhat qualified, it's a good idea to do some research on each of these jobs. The preeminent source for such job information is the *Dictionary of Occupational Titles*, or *DOT* (wave.net/upg/immigration/dot_index.html). This directory lists every conceivable job and provides excellent up-to-date information on duties and responsibilities, interactions with associates, and day-to-day assignments and tasks. These descriptions provide a thorough job analysis, but they do not consider the possible employers or the environments in which a job may be performed. So, although a position as public relations officer may be well defined in terms of duties and responsibilities, it does not explain the differences in doing public relations work in a college or a hospital or a factory or a bank. You will need to look somewhere else for work settings.

## Learn More About Possible Work Settings

After reading some job descriptions, you may choose to edit and revise your list of job titles once again, discarding those you feel are not suitable and keeping those that continue to hold your interest. Or you may wish to keep your list intact and see where these jobs may be located. For example, if you are interested in public relations and you appear to have those skills and the requisite education, you'll want to know what organizations do public relations. How can you find that out? How much income does someone in public relations make a year and what is the employment potential for the field of public relations?

To answer these and many other questions about your list of job titles, we recommend you try any of the following resources: *Careers Encyclopedia*, the professional societies and resources found throughout this book, *College to Career: The Guide to Job Opportunities*, and the *Occupational Outlook Handbook* (http://stats.bls.gov/ocohome.htm). Each of these resources, in a different way, will help to put the job titles you have selected into an employer context. Perhaps the most extensive discussion is found in the *Occupational Outlook Handbook*, which gives a thorough presentation of the nature of the work, the working conditions, employment statistics, training, other qualifications, and advancement possibilities as well as job outlook and earnings. Related occupations are also detailed, and a select bibliography is provided to help you find additional information.

Continuing with our public relations example, your search through these reference materials would teach you that the public relations jobs you find attractive are available in larger hospitals, financial institutions, most corporations (both consumer goods and industrial goods), media organizations, and colleges and universities.

# Networking

Networking is the process of deliberately establishing relationships to get career-related information or to alert potential employers that you are available for work. Networking is critically important to today's job seeker for two reasons: it will help you get the information you need, and it can help you find out about *all* of the available jobs.

### Get the Information You Need

Networkers will review your résumé and give you feedback on its effectiveness. They will talk about the job you are looking for and give you a candid appraisal of how they see your strengths and weaknesses. If they have a good sense of the industry or the employment sector for that job, you'll get their feelings on future trends in the industry as well. Some networkers will be very forthcoming about salaries, job-hunting techniques, and suggestions for your job search strategy. Many have been known to place calls right from the interview desk to friends and associates who might be interested in you. Each networker will make his or her own contribution, and each will be valuable.

Because organizations must evolve to adapt to current global market needs, the information provided by decision makers within various organizations will be critical to your success as a new job market entrant. For example, you might learn about the concept of virtual organizations from a networker. Virtual organizations coordinate economic activity to deliver value to customers by using resources outside the traditional boundaries of the organization. This concept is being discussed and implemented by chief executive officers of many organizations, including Ford Motor, Dell, and IBM. Networking can help you find out about this and other trends currently affecting the industries under your consideration.

### Find Out About All of the Available Jobs

Not every job that is available at this very moment is advertised for potential applicants to see. This is called the *hidden job market*. Only 15 to 20 percent of all jobs are formally advertised, which means that 80 to 85 percent of available jobs do not appear in published channels. Networking will help you become more knowledgeable about all the employment opportunities available during your job search period.

Although someone you might talk to today doesn't know of any openings within his or her organization, tomorrow or next week or next month an opening may occur. If you've taken the time to show an interest in and knowledge of their organization, if you've shown the company representative how you can help achieve organizational goals and that you can fit into the organization, you'll be one of the first candidates considered for the position.

### Networking: A Proactive Approach

Networking is a proactive rather than a reactive approach. You, as a job seeker, are expected to initiate a certain level of activity on your own behalf; you cannot afford to simply respond to jobs listed in the newspaper. Being proactive means building a network of contacts that includes informed and interested decision makers who will provide you with up-to-date knowledge of the current job market and increase your chances of finding out about employment opportunities appropriate for your interests, experience, and level of education. An old axiom of networking says, "You are only two phone calls away from the information you need." In other words, by talking to enough people, you will quickly come across someone who can offer you help.

## Preparing to Network

In deliberately establishing relationships, maximize your efforts by organizing your approach. Five specific areas in which you can organize your efforts include reviewing your self-assessment, reviewing your research on job sites and organizations, deciding who it is you want to talk to, keeping track of all your efforts, and creating your self-promotion tools.

### Review Your Self-Assessment

Your self-assessment is as important a tool in preparing to network as it has been in other aspects of your job search. You have carefully evaluated your personal traits, personal values, economic needs, longer-term goals, skill base, preferred skills, and underdeveloped skills. During the networking process you will be called upon to communicate what you know about yourself and relate it to the information or job you seek. Be sure to review the exercises that you completed in the self-assessment section of this book in preparation for networking. We've explained that you need to assess what skills you have acquired from your major that are of general value to an employer and to be ready to express those in ways employers can appreciate as useful in their own organizations.

## Review Research on Job Sites and Organizations

In addition, individuals assisting you will expect that you'll have at least some background information on the occupation or industry of interest to you. Refer to the appropriate sections of this book and other relevant publications to acquire the background information necessary for effective networking. They'll explain how to identify not only the job titles that might be of interest to you but also what kinds of organizations employ people to do that job. You will develop some sense of working conditions and expectations about duties and responsibilities—all of which will be of help in your networking interviews.

## Decide Who It Is You Want to Talk To

Networking cannot begin until you decide who it is that you want to talk to and, in general, what type of information you hope to gain from your contacts. Once you know this, it's time to begin developing a list of contacts. Five useful sources for locating contacts are described here.

*College Alumni Network.* Most colleges and universities have created a formal network of alumni and friends of the institution who are particularly interested in helping currently enrolled students and graduates of their alma mater gain employment-related information.

It is usually a simple process to make use of an alumni network. Visit your college's website and locate the alumni office and/or your career center. Either or both sites will have information about your school's alumni network. You'll be provided with information on shadowing experiences, geographic information, or those alumni offering job referrals. If you don't find what you're looking for, don't hesitate to phone or E-mail your career center and ask what they can do to help you connect with an alum.

Alumni networkers may provide some combination of the following services: day-long shadowing experiences, telephone interviews, in-person interviews, information on relocating to given geographic areas, internship information, suggestions on graduate school study, and job vacancy notices.

**Present and Former Supervisors.** If you believe you are on good terms with present or former job supervisors, they may be an excellent resource for providing information or directing you to appropriate resources that would have information related to your current interests and needs. Additionally, these supervisors probably belong to professional organizations that they might be willing to utilize to get information for you.

**Employers in Your Area.** Although you may be interested in working in a geographic location different from the one where you currently reside, don't overlook the value of the knowledge and contacts those around you are able to provide. Use the local telephone directory and newspaper to identify the types of organizations you are thinking of working for or professionals who have the kinds of jobs you are interested in. Recently, a call made to a local hospital's financial administrator for information on working in health-care financial administration yielded more pertinent information on training seminars, regional professional organizations, and potential employment sites than a national organization was willing to provide.

**Employers in Geographic Areas Where You Hope to Work.** If you are thinking about relocating, identifying prospective employers or informational contacts in the new location will be critical to your success. Here are some tips for online searching. First, use a "metasearch" engine to get the most out of your search. Metasearch engines combine several engines into one powerful tool. We frequently use dogpile.com and metasearch.com for this purpose. Try using the city and state as your keywords in a search. *New Haven, Connecticut* will bring you to the city's website with links to the chamber of commerce, member businesses, and other valuable resources. By using looksmart.com you can locate newspapers in any area, and they, too, can provide valuable insight before you relocate. Of course, both dogpile and metasearch can lead you to yellow and white page directories in areas you are considering.

**Professional Associations and Organizations.** Professional associations and organizations can provide valuable information in several areas: career paths that you might not have considered, qualifications relating to those career choices, publications that list current job openings, and workshops or seminars that will enhance your professional knowledge and skills. They can also be excellent sources for background information on given industries: their health, current problems, and future challenges.

There are several excellent resources available to help you locate professional associations and organizations that would have information to meet your needs. Two especially useful publications are the *Encyclopedia of Associations* and *National Trade and Professional Associations of the United States*.

### Keep Track of All Your Efforts

It can be difficult, almost impossible, to remember all the details related to each contact you make during the networking process, so you will want to develop a record-keeping system that works for you. Formalize this process by using your computer to keep a record of the people and organizations you want to contact. You can simply record the contact's name, address, and telephone number, and what information you hope to gain.

You could record this as a simple Word document and you could still use the "Find" function if you were trying to locate some data and could only recall the firm's name or the contact's name. If you're comfortable with database management and you have some database software on your computer, then you can put information at your fingertips even if you have only the zip code! The point here is not technological sophistication but good record keeping.

Once you have created this initial list, it will be helpful to keep more detailed information as you begin to actually make the contacts. Those details should include complete contact information, the date and content of each contact, names and information for additional networkers, and required follow-up. Don't forget to send a letter thanking your contact for his or her time! Your contact will appreciate your recall of details of your meetings and conversations, and the information will help you to focus your networking efforts.

### Create Your Self-Promotion Tools

There are two types of promotional tools that are used in the networking process. The first is a résumé and cover letter, and the second is a one-minute "infomercial," which may be given over the telephone or in person.

Techniques for writing an effective résumé and cover letter are discussed in Chapter 2. Once you have reviewed that material and prepared these important documents, you will have created one of your self-promotion tools.

The one-minute infomercial will demand that you begin tying your interests, abilities, and skills to the people or organizations you want to network with. Think about your goal for making the contact to help you understand what you should say about yourself. You should be able to express yourself easily and convincingly. If, for example, you are contacting an alumnus of your institution to obtain the names of possible employment sites in a distant city, be prepared to discuss why you are interested in moving to that location, the types of jobs you are interested in, and the skills and abilities you possess that will make you a qualified candidate.

To create a meaningful one-minute infomercial, write it out, practice it as if it will be a spoken presentation, rewrite it, and practice it again if necessary until expressing yourself comes easily and is convincing.

Here's a simplified example of an infomercial for use over the telephone:

---

Hello, Mr. Porter. My name is Ann Dalton. I recently graduated from State College and hope to begin a career in zoology. I was a biology major and believe that I have many of the skills needed in zoology, such as analytical thinking, researching, and computer skills. I can work independently or in a team, which I understand is a real advantage in this field.

Mr. Porter, I'm calling because I still need more information about zoology. I hope that you'll be willing to meet with me for about half an hour to share your views on the profession. I think discussing some of the career options with you might help me to decide which would be the best path for me to take.

I would greatly appreciate it if you would be willing to do this for me. I can be available to meet you at your convenience.

---

It very well may happen that your employer contact wishes you to communicate by E-mail. The infomercial quoted above could easily be rewritten for an E-mail message. You should "cut and paste" your résumé right into the E-mail text itself.

Other effective self-promotion tools include portfolios for those in the arts, writing professions, or teaching. Portfolios show examples of work, photographs of projects or classroom activities, or certificates and credentials that are job related. There may not be an opportunity to use the portfolio during an interview, and it is not something that should be left with the organization. It is designed to be explained and displayed by the creator. However, during some networking meetings, there may be an opportunity to illustrate a point or strengthen a qualification by exhibiting the portfolio.

# Beginning the Networking Process

### Set the Tone for Your Communications

It can be useful to establish "tone words" for any communications you embark upon. Before making your first telephone call or writing your first letter, decide what you want the person to think of you. If you are networking to try to obtain a job, your tone words might include descriptors such as *genuine*, *informed*, and *self-knowledgeable*. When you're trying to acquire information, your tone words may have a slightly different focus, such as *courteous*, *organized*, *focused*, and *well-spoken*. Use the tone words you establish for your contacts to guide you through the networking process.

### Honestly Express Your Intentions

When contacting individuals, it is important to be honest about your reasons for making the contact. Establish your purpose in your own mind and be able and ready to articulate it concisely. Determine an initial agenda, whether it be informational questioning or self-promotion, present it to your contact, and be ready to respond immediately. If you don't adequately prepare before initiating your overture, you may find yourself at a disadvantage if you're asked to immediately begin your informational interview or self-promotion during the first phone conversation or visit.

### Start Networking Within Your Circle of Confidence

Once you have organized your approach—by utilizing specific researching methods, creating a system for keeping track of the people you will contact, and developing effective self-promotion tools—you are ready to begin networking. The best way to begin networking is by talking with a group of people you trust and feel comfortable with. This group is usually made up of your family, friends, and career counselors. No matter who is in this inner circle, they will have a special interest in seeing you succeed in your job search. In addition, because they will be easy to talk to, you should try taking some risks in terms of practicing your information-seeking approach. Gain confidence in talking about the strengths you bring to an organization and the underdeveloped skills you feel hinder your candidacy. Be sure to review the section on self-assessment for tips on approaching each of these areas. Ask for critical but constructive feedback from the people in your circle of confidence on the letters you write and the one-minute infomercial you have developed. Evaluate whether you want to make the changes they suggest, then practice the changes on others within this circle.

## Stretch the Boundaries of Your Networking Circle of Confidence

Once you have refined the promotional tools you will use to accomplish your networking goals, you will want to make additional contacts. Because you will not know most of these people, it will be a less comfortable activity to undertake. The practice that you gained with your inner circle of trusted friends should have prepared you to now move outside of that comfort zone.

It is said that any information a person needs is only two phone calls away, but the information cannot be gained until you (1) make a reasonable guess about who might have the information you need and (2) pick up the telephone to make the call. Using your network list that includes alumni, instructors, supervisors, employers, and associations, you can begin preparing your list of questions that will allow you to get the information you need.

## Prepare the Questions You Want to Ask

Networkers can provide you with the insider's perspective on any given field and you can ask them questions that you might not want to ask in an interview. For example, you can ask them to describe the more repetitious or mundane parts of the job or ask them for a realistic idea of salary expectations. Be sure to prepare your questions ahead of time so that you are organized and efficient.

## Be Prepared to Answer Some Questions

To communicate effectively, you must anticipate questions that will be asked of you by the networkers you contact. Revisit the self-assessment process you undertook and the research you've done so that you can effortlessly respond to questions about your short- and long-term goals and the kinds of jobs you are most interested in pursuing.

## General Networking Tips

*Make Every Contact Count.* Setting the tone for each interaction is critical. Approaches that will help you communicate in an effective way include politeness, being appreciative of time provided to you, and being prepared and thorough. Remember, *everyone* within an organization has a circle of influence, so be prepared to interact effectively with each person you encounter in the networking process, including secretarial and support staff. Many information or job seekers have thwarted their own efforts by being rude to some individuals they encountered as they networked because they made the incorrect assumption that certain persons were unimportant.

Sometimes your contacts may be surprised at their ability to help you. After meeting and talking with you, they might think they have not offered much in the way of help. A day or two later, however, they may make a contact that would be useful to you and refer you to that person.

**With Each Contact, Widen Your Circle of Networkers.** Always leave an informational interview with the names of at least two more people who can help you get the information or job that you are seeking. Don't be shy about asking for additional contacts; networking is all about increasing the number of people you can interact with to achieve your goals.

**Make Your Own Decisions.** As you talk with different people and get answers to the questions you pose, you may hear conflicting information or get conflicting suggestions. Your job is to listen to these "experts" and decide what information and which suggestions will help you achieve *your* goals. Only implement those suggestions that you believe will work for you.

## Shutting Down Your Network

As you achieve the goals that motivated your networking activity—getting the information you need or the job you want—the time will come to inactivate all or parts of your network. As you do, be sure to tell your primary supporters about your change in status. Call or write to each one of them and give them as many details about your new status as you feel is necessary to maintain a positive relationship.

Because a network takes on a life of its own, activity undertaken on your behalf will continue even after you cease your efforts. As you get calls or are contacted in some fashion, be sure to inform these networkers about your change in status, and thank them for assistance they have provided.

Information on the latest employment trends indicates that workers will change jobs or careers several times in their lifetime. Networking, then, will be a critical aspect in the span of your professional life. If you carefully and thoughtfully conduct your networking activities during your job search, you will have a solid foundation of experience when you need to network the next time around.

## Where Are These Jobs, Anyway?

Having a list of job titles that you've designed around your own career interests and skills is an excellent beginning. It means you've really thought about who you are and what you are presenting to the employment market. It has caused you to think seriously about the most appealing environments to work in, and you have identified some employer types that represent these environments.

The research and the thinking that you've done thus far will be used again and again. They will be helpful in writing your résumé and cover letters, in talking about yourself on the telephone to prospective employers, and in answering interview questions.

Now is a good time to begin to narrow the field of job titles and employment sites down to some specific employers to initiate the employment contact.

### Find Out Which Employers Hire People Like You

This section will provide tips, techniques, and specific resources for developing an actual list of specific employers that can be used to make contacts. It is only an outline that you must be prepared to tailor to your own particular needs and according to what you bring to the job search. Once again, it is important to communicate with others along the way exactly what you're looking for and what your goals are for the research you're doing. Librarians, employers, career counselors, friends, friends of friends, business contacts, and bookstore staff will all have helpful information on geographically specific and new resources to aid you in locating employers who'll hire you.

### Identify Information Resources

Your interview wardrobe and your new résumé might have put a dent in your wallet, but the resources you'll need to pursue your job search are available for free. The categories of information detailed here are not hard to find and are yours for the browsing.

Numerous resources described in this section will help you identify actual employers. Use all of them or any others that you identify as available in your geographic area. As you become experienced in this process, you'll quickly figure out which information sources are helpful and which are not. If you live in a rural area, a well-planned day trip to a major city that includes a college career office, a large college or city library, state and federal employment centers, a chamber of commerce office, and a well-stocked bookstore can produce valuable results.

There are many excellent resources available to help you identify actual job sites. They are categorized into employer directories (usually indexed by product lines and geographic location), geographically based directories (designed to highlight particular cities, regions, or states), career-specific directories (e.g., *Sports MarketPlace*, which lists tens of thousands of firms involved with sports), periodicals and newspapers, targeted job posting publications, and videos. This is by no means meant to be a complete treatment of resources but rather a starting point for identifying useful resources.

Working from the more general references to highly specific resources, we provide a basic list to help you begin your search. Many of these you'll find easily available. In some cases reference librarians and others will suggest even better materials for your particular situation. Start to create your own customized bibliography of job search references.

**Geographically Based Directories.** The Job Bank series published by Bob Adams, Inc. (aip.com) contains detailed entries on each area's major employers, including business activity, address, phone number, and hiring contact name. Many listings specify educational backgrounds being sought in potential employees. Each volume contains a solid discussion of each city's or state's major employment sectors. Organizations are also indexed by industry. Job Bank volumes are available for the following places: Atlanta, Boston, Chicago, Dallas–Ft. Worth, Denver, Detroit, Florida, Houston, Los Angeles, Minneapolis, New York, Ohio, Philadelphia, San Francisco, Seattle, St. Louis, Washington, D.C., and other cities throughout the Northwest.

*National Job Bank* (careercity.com) lists employers in every state, along with contact names and commonly hired job categories. Included are many small companies often overlooked by other directories. Companies are also indexed by industry. This publication provides information on educational backgrounds sought and lists company benefits.

**Periodicals and Newspapers.** Several sources are available to help you locate which journals or magazines carry job advertisements in your field. Other resources help you identify opportunities in other parts of the country.

- *Where the Jobs Are: A Comprehensive Directory of 1200 Journals Listing Career Opportunities*
- *Corptech Fast 5000 Company Locator*
- *National Ad Search* (nationaladsearch.com)
- *The Federal Jobs Digest* (jobsfed.com) and *Federal Career Opportunities*
- *World Chamber of Commerce Directory* (chamberofcommerce.org)

This list is certainly not exhaustive; use it to begin your job search work.

**Targeted Job Posting Publications.** Although the resources that follow are national in scope, they are either targeted to one medium of contact (telephone), focused on specific types of jobs, or less comprehensive than the sources previously listed.

- *Job Hotlines USA* (careers.org/topic/01_002.html)
- *The Job Hunter* (jobhunter.com)
- *Current Jobs for Graduates* (graduatejobs.com)
- *Environmental Opportunities* (ecojobs.com)
- *Y National Vacancy List* (ymcahrm.ns.ca/employed/jobleads.html)
- *ARTSearch*
- *Community Jobs*
- *National Association of Colleges and Employers: Job Choices series*
- *National Association of Colleges and Employers* (naceweb.org)

**Videos.** You may be one of the many job seekers who likes to get information via a medium other than paper. Many career libraries, public libraries, and career centers in libraries carry an assortment of videos that will help you learn new techniques and get information helpful in the job search.

## Locate Information Resources

Throughout these introductory chapters, we have continually referred you to various websites for information on everything from job listings to career information. Using the Web gives you a mobility at your computer that you don't enjoy if you rely solely on books or newspapers or printed journals. Moreover, material on the Web, if the site is maintained, can be the most up-to-date information available.

You'll eventually identify the information resources that work best for you, but make certain you've covered the full range of resources before you begin to rely on a smaller list. Here's a short list of informational sites that many job seekers find helpful:

- Public and college libraries
- College career centers
- Bookstores
- The Internet
- Local and state government personnel offices
- Career/job fairs

Each one of these sites offers a collection of resources that will help you get the information you need.

As you meet and talk with service professionals at all these sites, be sure to let them know what you're doing. Inform them of your job search, what you've already accomplished, and what you're looking for. The more people who know you're job seeking, the greater the possibility that someone will have information or know someone who can help you along your way.

# 4

# Interviewing and Job Offer Considerations

Certainly, there can be no one part of the job search process more fraught with anxiety and worry than the interview. Yet seasoned job seekers welcome the interview and will often say, "Just get me an interview and I'm on my way!" They understand that the interview is crucial to the hiring process and equally crucial for them, as job candidates, to have the opportunity of a personal dialogue to add to what the employer may already have learned from the résumé, cover letter, and telephone conversations.

Believe it or not, the interview is to be welcomed, and even enjoyed! It is a perfect opportunity for you, the candidate, to sit down with an employer and express yourself and display who you are and what you want. Of course, it takes thought and planning and a little strategy; after all, it *is* a job interview! But it can be a positive, if not pleasant, experience and one you can look back on and feel confident about your performance and effort.

For many new job seekers, a job, any job, seems a wonderful thing. But seasoned interview veterans know that the job interview is an important step for both sides—the employer and the candidate—to see what each has to offer and whether there is going to be a "fit" of personalities, work styles, and attitudes. And it is this concept of balance in the interview, that both sides have important parts to play, that holds the key to success in mastering this aspect of the job search strategy.

Try to think of the interview as a conversation between two interested and equal partners. You both have important, even vital, information to deliver and to learn. Of course, there's no denying the employer has some leverage, especially in the initial interview for recruitment or any interview scheduled by the candidate and not the recruiter. That should not prevent the interviewee from seeking to play an equal part in what should be a fair exchange of information. Too often the untutored candidate allows the interview to become one-sided. The employer asks all the questions and the candidate simply responds. The ideal would be for two mutually interested parties to sit down and discuss possibilities for each. This is a conversation of significance, and it requires preparation, thought about the tone of the interview, and planning of the nature and details of the information to be exchanged.

## Preparing for the Interview

The length of most initial interviews is about thirty minutes. Given the brevity, the information that is exchanged ought to be important. The candidate should be delivering material that the employer cannot discover on the résumé, and in turn, the candidate should be learning things about the employer that he or she could not otherwise find out. After all, if you have only thirty minutes, why waste time on information that is already published? The information exchanged is more than just factual, and both sides will learn much from what they see of each other, as well. How the candidate looks, speaks, and acts are important to the employer. The employer's attention to the interview and awareness of the candidate's résumé, the setting, and the quality of information presented are important to the candidate.

Just as the employer has every right to be disappointed when a prospect is late for the interview, looks unkempt, and seems ill-prepared to answer fairly standard questions, the candidate may be disappointed with an interviewer who isn't ready for the meeting, hasn't learned the basic résumé facts, and is constantly interrupted by telephone calls. In either situation there's good reason to feel let down.

There are many elements to a successful interview, and some of them are not easy to describe or prepare for. Sometimes there is just a chemistry between interviewer and interviewee that brings out the best in both, and a good exchange takes place. But there is much the candidate can do to pave the way for success in terms of his or her résumé, personal appearance, goals, and interview strategy—each of which we will discuss. However, none of this preparation is as important as the time and thought the candidate gives to personal self-assessment.

### Self-Assessment
Neither a stunning résumé nor an expensive, well-tailored suit can compensate for candidates who do not know what they want, where they are going,

or why they are interviewing with a particular employer. Self-assessment, the process by which we begin to know and acknowledge our own particular blend of education, experiences, needs, and goals, is not something that can be sorted out the weekend before a major interview. Of all the elements of interview preparation, this one requires the longest lead time and cannot be faked.

Because the time allotted for most interviews is brief, it is all the more important for job candidates to understand and express succinctly why they are there and what they have to offer. This is not a time for undue modesty (or for braggadocio either); it is a time for a compelling, reasoned statement of why you feel that you and this employer might make a good match. It means you have to have thought about your skills, interests, and attributes; related those to your life experiences and your own history of challenges and opportunities; and determined what that indicates about your strengths, preferences, values, and areas needing further development.

If you need some assistance with self-assessment issues, refer to Chapter 1. Included are suggested exercises that can be done as needed, such as making up an experiential diary and extracting obvious strengths and weaknesses from past experiences. These simple assignments will help you look at past activities as collections of tasks with accompanying skills and responsibilities. Don't overlook your high school or college career office. Many offer personal counseling on self-assessment issues and may provide testing instruments such as the *Myers-Briggs Type Indicator (MBTI)*, the *Harrington-O'Shea Career Decision-Making System (CDM)*, the *Strong Interest Inventory (SII)*, or any other of a wide selection of assessment tools that can help you clarify some of these issues prior to the interview stage of your job search.

## The Résumé

Résumé preparation has been discussed in detail, and some basic examples were provided. In this section we want to concentrate on how best to use your résumé in the interview. In most cases the employer will have seen the résumé prior to the interview, and, in fact, it may well have been the quality of that résumé that secured the interview opportunity.

An interview is a conversation, however, and not an exercise in reading. So, if the employer hasn't seen your résumé and you have brought it along to the interview, wait until asked or until the end of the interview to offer it. Otherwise, you may find yourself staring at the back of your résumé and simply answering "yes" and "no" to a series of questions drawn from that document.

Sometimes an interviewer is not prepared and does not know or recall the contents of the résumé and may use the résumé to a greater or lesser degree as a "prompt" during the interview. It is for you to judge what that may indicate about the individual performing the interview or the employer. If your interviewer seems surprised by the scheduled meeting, relies on the résumé to an inordinate degree, and seems otherwise unfamiliar with your background, this lack of preparation for the hiring process could well be a symptom of general management disorganization or may simply be the result of poor planning on the part of one individual. It is your responsibility as a potential employee to be aware of these signals and make your decisions accordingly.

---

In any event, it is perfectly acceptable for you to get the conversation back to a more interpersonal style by saying something like, "Mr. Smith, you might be interested in some recent experience I gained in an internship that is not detailed on my résumé. May I tell you about it?" This can return the interview to two people talking to each other, not one reading and the other responding.

---

By all means, bring at least one copy of your résumé to the interview. Occasionally, at the close of an interview, an interviewer will express an interest in circulating a résumé to several departments, and you could then offer the copy you brought. Sometimes, an interview appointment provides an opportunity to meet others in the organization who may express an interest in you and your background, and it may be helpful to follow up with a copy of your résumé. Our best advice, however, is to keep it out of sight until needed or requested.

## Employer Information

Whether your interview is for graduate school admission, an overseas corporate position, or a position with a local company, it is important to know something about the employer or the organization. Keeping in mind that the interview is relatively brief and that you will hopefully have other interviews with other organizations, it is important to keep your research in proportion. If secondary interviews are called for, you will have additional time to do further research. For the first interview, it is helpful to know the organization's mission, goals, size, scope of operations, and so forth. Your research may uncover recent areas of challenge or particular successes that may help to fuel the interview. Use the "What Do They Call the Job You Want?" section of Chapter 3, your library, and your career or guidance office to help you locate this information in the most efficient way possible. Don't be shy in asking advice of these counseling and guidance professionals on how best to spend your preparation time. With some practice, you'll soon learn how much information is enough and which kinds of information are most useful to you.

## Interview Content

We've already discussed how it can help to think of the interview as an important conversation—one that, as with any conversation, you want to find pleasant and interesting and to leave you with a good feeling. But because this conversation is especially important, the information that's exchanged is critical to its success. What do you want them to know about you? What do you need to know about them? What interview technique do you need to particularly pay attention to? How do you want to manage the close of the interview? What steps will follow in the hiring process?

Except for the professional interviewer, most of us find interviewing stressful and anxiety-provoking. Developing a strategy before you begin interviewing will help you relieve some stress and anxiety. One particular strategy that has worked for many and may work for you is interviewing by objective. Before you interview, write down three to five goals you would like to achieve for that interview. They may be technique goals: smile a little more, have a firmer handshake, be sure to ask about the next stage in the interview process before leaving. They may be content-oriented goals: find out about the company's current challenges and opportunities; be sure to speak of your recent research, writing experiences, or foreign travel. Whatever your goals, jot down a few of them as goals for each interview.

Most people find that in trying to achieve these few goals, their interviewing technique becomes more organized and focused. After the interview, the most common question friends and family ask is "How did it go?" With this technique, you have an indication of whether you met *your* goals for the meeting, not just some vague idea of how it went. Chances are, if you accomplished what you wanted to, it improved the quality of the entire interview. As you continue to interview, you will want to revise your goals to continue improving your interview skills.

Now, add to the concept of the significant conversation the idea of a beginning, a middle, and a closing and you will have two thoughts that will give your interview a distinctive character. Be sure to make your introduction warm and cordial. Say your full name (and if it's a difficult-to-pronounce name, help the interviewer to pronounce it) and make certain you know your interviewer's name and how to pronounce it. Most interviews begin with some "soft talk" about the weather, chat about the candidate's trip to the interview site, or national events. This is done as a courtesy to relax both you and the interviewer, to get you talking, and to generally try to defuse the atmosphere of excessive tension. Try to be yourself, engage in the conversation, and don't try to second-guess the interviewer. This is simply what it appears to be—casual conversation.

Once you and the interviewer move on to exchange more serious information in the middle part of the interview, the two most important concerns become your ability to handle challenging questions and your success at asking meaningful ones. Interviewer questions will probably fall into one of three categories: personal assessment and career direction, academic assessment, and knowledge of the employer. Here are a few examples of questions in each category:

## Personal Assessment and Career Direction
1. What motivates you to put forth your best effort?
2. What do you consider to be your greatest strengths and weaknesses?
3. What qualifications do you have that make you think you will be successful in this career?

## Academic Assessment
1. What led you to choose your major?
2. What subjects did you like best and least? Why?
3. How has your college experience prepared you for this career?

## Knowledge of the Employer
1. What do you think it takes to be successful in an organization like ours?
2. In what ways do you think you can make a contribution to our organization?
3. Why did you choose to seek a position with this organization?

The interviewer wants a response to each question but is also gauging your enthusiasm, preparedness, and willingness to communicate. In each response you should provide some information about yourself that can be related to the employer's needs. A common mistake is to give too much information. Answer each question completely, but be careful not to run on too long with extensive details or examples.

## Questions About Underdeveloped Skills

Most employers interview people who have met some minimum criteria of education and experience. They interview candidates to see who they are, to learn what kind of personality they exhibit, and to get some sense of how this person might fit into the existing organization. It may be that you are asked about skills the employer hopes to find and that you have not documented. Maybe it's grant-writing experience, knowledge of the European political system, or a knowledge of the film world.

To questions about skills and experiences you don't have, answer honestly and forthrightly and try to offer some additional information about skills you do have. For example, perhaps the employer is disappointed you have no grant-writing experience. An honest answer may be as follows:

*No, unfortunately, I was never in a position to acquire those skills. I do understand something of the complexities of the grant-writing process and feel confident that my attention to detail, careful reading skills, and strong writing would make grants a wonderful challenge in a new job. I think I could get up on the learning curve quickly.*

The employer hears an honest admission of lack of experience but is reassured by some specific skill details that do relate to grant writing and a confident manner that suggests enthusiasm and interest in a challenge.

For many students, questions about their possible contribution to an employer's organization can prove challenging. Because your education has probably not included specific training for a job, you need to review your academic record and select capabilities you have developed in your major that an employer can appreciate. For example, perhaps you read well and can analyze and condense what you've read into smaller, more focused pieces. That could be valuable. Or maybe you did some serious research and you know you have valuable investigative skills. Your public speaking might be highly developed and you might use visual aids appropriately and effectively. Or maybe your skill at correspondence, memos, and messages is effective. Whatever it is, you must take it out of the academic context and put it into a new, employer-friendly context so your interviewer can best judge how you could help the organization.

Exhibiting knowledge of the organization will, without a doubt, show the interviewer that you are interested enough in the available position to have done some legwork in preparation for the interview. Remember, it is not necessary to know every detail of the organization's history but rather to have a general knowledge about why it is in business and how the industry is faring.

Sometime during the interview, generally after the midway point, you'll be asked if you have any questions for the interviewer. Your questions will tell the employer much about your attitude and your desire to understand the organization's expectations so you can compare them to your own strengths. The following are just a few questions you might want to ask:

1. What is the communication style of the organization? (meetings, memos, and so forth)
2. What would a typical day in this position be like for me?
3. What have been some of the interesting challenges and opportunities your organization has recently faced?

Most interviews draw to a natural closing point, so be careful not to prolong the discussion. At a signal from the interviewer, wind up your presentation, express your appreciation for the opportunity, and be sure to ask what the next stage in the process will be. When can you expect to hear from them? Will they be conducting second-tier interviews? If you are interested and haven't heard, would they mind a phone call? Be sure to collect a business card with the name and phone number of your interviewer. On your way out, you might have an opportunity to pick up organizational literature you haven't seen before.

With the right preparation—a thorough self-assessment, professional clothing, and employer information—you'll be able to set and achieve the goals you have established for the interview process.

## Interview Follow-Up

Quite often there is a considerable time lag between interviewing for a position and being hired or, in the case of the networker, between your phone call or letter to a possible contact and the opportunity of a meeting. This can be frustrating. "Why aren't they contacting me?" "I thought I'd get another interview, but no one has telephoned." "Am I out of the running?" You don't know what is happening.

### Consider the Differing Perspectives

Of course, there is another perspective—that of the networker or hiring organization. Organizations are complex, with multiple tasks that need to be accomplished each day. Hiring is a discrete activity that does not occur as frequently as other job assignments. The hiring process might have to take second place to other, more immediate organizational needs. Although it may be very important to you, and it is certainly ultimately significant to the employer, other issues such as fiscal management, planning and product development, employer vacation periods, or financial constraints may prevent an organization or individual within that organization from acting on your employment or your request for information as quickly as you or they would prefer.

## Use Your Communication Skills

Good communication is essential here to resolve any anxieties, and the responsibility is on you, the job or information seeker. Too many job seekers and networkers offer as an excuse that they don't want to "bother" the organization by writing letters or calling. Let us assure you here and now, once and for all, that if you are troubling an organization by over-communicating, someone will indicate that situation to you quite clearly. If not, you can only assume you are a worthwhile prospect and the employer appreciates being reminded of your availability and interest. Let's look at follow-up practices in the job interview process and the networking situation separately.

## Following Up on the Employment Interview

A brief thank-you note following an interview is an excellent and polite way to begin a series of follow-up communications with a potential employer with whom you have interviewed and want to remain in touch. It should be just that—a thank-you for a good meeting. If you failed to mention some fact or experience during your interview that you think might add to your candidacy, you may use this note to do that. However, this should be essentially a note whose overall tone is appreciative and, if appropriate, indicative of a continuing interest in pursuing any opportunity that may exist with that organization. It is one of the few pieces of business correspondence that may be handwritten, but always use plain, good-quality, standard-size paper.

If, however, at this point you are no longer interested in the employer, the thank-you note is an appropriate time to indicate that. You are under no obligation to identify any reason for not continuing to pursue employment with that organization, but if you are so inclined to indicate your professional reasons (pursuing other employers more akin to your interests, looking for greater income production than this employer can provide, a different geographic location), you certainly may. It should not be written with an eye to negotiation, for it will not be interpreted as such.

As part of your interview closing, you should have taken the initiative to establish lines of communication for continuing information about your candidacy. If you asked permission to telephone, wait a week following your thank-you note, then telephone your contact simply to inquire how things are progressing on your employment status. The feedback you receive here should be taken at face value. If your interviewer simply has no information, he or she will tell you so and indicate whether you should call again and when. Don't be discouraged if this should continue over some period of time.

If during this time something occurs that you think improves or changes your candidacy (some new qualification or experience you may have had), including any offers from other organizations, by all means telephone or write to inform the employer about this. In the case of an offer from a competing but less desirable or equally desirable organization, telephone your contact, explain what has happened, express your real interest in the organization, and inquire whether some determination on your employment might be made before you must respond to this other offer. An organization that is truly interested in you may be moved to make a decision about your candidacy. Equally possible is the scenario in which they are not yet ready to make a decision and so advise you to take the offer that has been presented. Again, you have no ethical alternative but to deal with the information presented in a straightforward manner.

When accepting other employment, be sure to contact any employers still actively considering you and inform them of your new job. Thank them graciously for their consideration. There are many other job seekers out there just like you who will benefit from having their candidacy improved when others bow out of the race. Who knows, you might at some future time have occasion to interact professionally with one of the organizations with which you sought employment. How embarrassing it would be to have someone remember you as the candidate who failed to notify them that you were taking a job elsewhere!

In all of your follow-up communications, keep good notes of whom you spoke with, when you called, and any instructions that were given about return communications. This will prevent any misunderstandings and provide you with good records of what has transpired.

## Job Offer Considerations

For many recent college graduates, the thrill of their first job and, for some, the most substantial regular income they have ever earned seems an excess of good fortune coming at once. To question that first income or to be critical in any way of the conditions of employment at the time of the initial offer seems like looking a gift horse in the mouth. It doesn't seem to occur to many new hires even to attempt to negotiate any aspect of their first job. And, as many employers who deal with entry-level jobs for recent college graduates will readily confirm, the reality is that there simply isn't much movement in salary available to these new college recruits. The entry-level hire generally does not have an employment track record on a professional level to provide any leverage for negotiation. Real negotiations on salary, benefits, retirement provisions, and so forth come to those with significant employment records at higher income levels.

Of course, the job offer is more than just money. It can be composed of geographic assignment, duties and responsibilities, training, benefits, health and medical insurance, educational assistance, car allowance or company vehicle, and a host of other items. All of this is generally detailed in the formal letter that presents the final job offer. In most cases this is a follow-up to a personal phone call from the employer representative who has been principally responsible for your hiring process.

That initial telephone offer is certainly binding as a verbal agreement, but most firms follow up with a detailed letter outlining the most significant parts of your employment contract. You may, of course, choose to respond immediately at the time of the telephone offer (which would be considered a binding oral contract), but you will also be required to formally answer the letter of offer with a letter of acceptance, restating the salient elements of the employer's description of your position, salary, and benefits. This ensures that both parties are clear on the terms and conditions of employment and remuneration and any other outstanding aspects of the job offer.

### Is This the Job You Want?

Most new employees will respond affirmatively in writing, glad to be in the position to accept employment. If you've worked hard to get the offer and the job market is tight, other offers may not be in sight, so you will say, "Yes, I accept!" What is important here is that the job offer you accept be one that does fit your particular needs, values, and interests as you've outlined them in your self-assessment process. Moreover, it should be a job that will not only use your skills and education but also challenge you to develop new skills and talents.

Jobs are sometimes accepted too hastily, for the wrong reasons, and without proper scrutiny by the applicant. For example, an individual might readily accept a sales job only to find the continual rejection by potential clients unendurable. An office worker might realize within weeks the constraints of a desk job and yearn for more activity. Employment is an important part of our lives. It is, for most of our adult lives, our most continuous productive activity. We want to make good choices based on the right criteria.

If you have a low tolerance for risk, a job based on commission will certainly be very anxiety-provoking. If being near your family is important, issues of relocation could present a decision crisis for you. If you're an adventurous person, a job with frequent travel would provide needed excitement and be very desirable. The importance of income, the need to continue your education, your personal health situation—all of these have an impact on whether the job you are considering will ultimately meet your needs. Unless you've spent some time understanding and thinking about these issues, it will be difficult to evaluate offers you do receive.

More important, if you make a decision that you cannot tolerate and feel you must leave that job, you will then have both unemployment and self-esteem issues to contend with. These will combine to make the next job search tough going, indeed. So make your acceptance a carefully considered decision.

## Negotiate Your Offer

It may be that there is some aspect of your job offer that is not particularly attractive to you. Perhaps there is no relocation allotment to help you move your possessions, and this presents some financial hardship for you. It may be that the health insurance is less than you had hoped. Your initial assignment may be different from what you expected, either in its location or in the duties and responsibilities that comprise it. Or it may simply be that the salary is less than you anticipated. Other considerations may be your official starting date of employment, vacation time, evening hours, dates of training programs or schools, and other concerns.

If you are considering not accepting the job because of some item or items in the job offer "package" that do not meet your needs, you should know that most employers emphatically wish that you would bring that issue to their attention. It may be that the employer can alter it to make the offer more agreeable for you. In some cases it cannot be changed. In any event the employer would generally like to have the opportunity to try to remedy a difficulty rather than risk losing a good potential employee over an issue that might have been resolved. After all, they have spent time and funds in securing your services, and they certainly deserve an opportunity to resolve any possible differences.

Honesty is the best approach in discussing any objections or uneasiness you might have over the employer's offer. Having received your formal offer in writing, contact your employer representative and indicate your particular dissatisfaction in a straightforward manner. For example, you might explain that while you are very interested in being employed by this organization, the salary (or any other benefit) is less than you have determined you require. State the terms you need, and listen to the response. You may be asked to put this in writing, or you may be asked to hold off until the firm can decide on a response. If you are dealing with a senior representative of the organization, one who has been involved in hiring for some time, you may get an immediate response or a solid indication of possible outcomes.

Perhaps the issue is one of relocation. Your initial assignment is in the Midwest, and because you had indicated a strong West Coast preference, you are surprised at the actual assignment. You might simply indicate that while you understand the need for the company to assign you based on its needs, you are disappointed and had hoped to be placed on the West Coast. You could inquire if that were still possible and, if not, would it be reasonable to expect a West Coast relocation in the future.

If your request is presented in a reasonable way, most employers will not see this as jeopardizing your offer. If they can agree to your proposal, they will. If not, they will simply tell you so, and you may choose to continue your candidacy with them or remove yourself from consideration. The choice will be up to you.

Some firms will adjust benefits within their parameters to meet the candidate's need if at all possible. If a candidate requires a relocation cost allowance, he or she may be asked to forgo tuition benefits for the first year to accomplish this adjustment. An increase in life insurance may be adjusted by some other benefit trade-off; perhaps a family dental plan is not needed. In these decisions you are called upon, sometimes under time pressure, to know how you value these issues and how important each is to you.

Many employers find they are more comfortable negotiating for candidates who have unique qualifications or who bring especially needed expertise to the organization. Employers hiring large numbers of entry-level college graduates may be far more reluctant to accommodate any changes in offer conditions. They are well supplied with candidates with similar education and experience so that if rejected by one candidate, they can draw new candidates from an ample labor pool.

## Compare Offers

The condition of the economy, the job seeker's academic major and particular geographic job market, and individual needs and demands for certain employment conditions may not provide more than one job offer at a time. Some job seekers may feel that no reasonable offer should go unaccepted for the simple fear there won't be another.

In a tough job market, or if the job you seek is not widely available, or when your job search goes on too long and becomes difficult to sustain financially and emotionally, it may be necessary to accept an inferior offer. The alternative is continued unemployment. Even here, when you feel you don't have a choice, you can at least understand that in accepting this particular offer, there may be limitations and conditions you don't appreciate. At the time of acceptance, there were no other alternatives, but you can begin to use that position to gain the experience and talent to move toward a more attractive position.

Sometimes, however, more than one offer is received, and the candidate has the luxury of choice. If the job seeker knows what he or she wants and has done the necessary self-assessment honestly and thoroughly, it may be clear that one of the offers conforms more closely to those expressed wants and needs.

However, if, as so often happens, the offers are similar in terms of conditions and salary, the question then becomes which organization might provide the necessary climate, opportunities, and advantages for your professional development and growth. This is the time when solid employer research and astute questioning during the interviews really pays off. How much did you learn about the employer through your own research and skillful questioning? When the interviewer asked during the interview "Do you have any questions?" did you ask the kinds of questions that would help resolve a choice between one organization and another? Just as an employer must decide among numerous applicants, so must the applicant learn to assess the potential employer. Both are partners in the job search.

## Reneging on an Offer

An especially disturbing occurrence for employers and career counseling professionals is when a job seeker formally (either orally or by written contract) accepts employment with one organization and later reneges on the agreement and goes with another employer.

There are all kinds of rationalizations offered for this unethical behavior. None of them satisfies. The sad irony is that what the job seeker is willing to do to the employer—make a promise and then break it—he or she would be outraged to have done to him- or herself: have the job offer pulled. It is a very bad way to begin a career. It suggests the individual has not taken the time to do the necessary self-assessment and self-awareness exercises to think and judge critically. The new offer taken may, in fact, be no better or worse than the one refused. You should be aware that there have been incidents of legal action following job candidates' reneging on an offer. This adds a very sour note to what should be a harmonious beginning of a lifelong adventure.

# PART TWO

# THE CAREER PATHS

# 5

# Introduction to Biology Career Paths

With so much diversity in the field of biology, choosing the right career path can sometimes present quite a dilemma. The level of education you possess, the area of interest that consumes you, the amount of time you are willing to devote to study, and the setting in which you choose to work will all contribute toward determining the right career path for you to take.

But before you commit yourself to a path, explore it first. And if possible, begin that exploration early, with the diverse educational programs offered around the country.

## Choosing the Right Biology Program

There are almost as many different names and focuses for biology programs as there are job possibilities. Universities often divide their departments into particular areas of concentration, and it's important for the incoming student to know the department's focus before applying. The University of Colorado at Boulder, for example, has two programs: EPO (environmental, populations, organisms) and MCDB (molecular, cellular, developmental biology). This division is made clear so students who want to study microbes won't end up accidentally in a "Birds of North America" course, and the future zoologist won't be trying to learn how to conduct gel electrophoresis.

Other universities offer integrated programs. For example, at the University of California at Berkeley the following related but separate fields are offered in one department: botany, evolutionary biology, ecology, marine biology, paleontology, and zoology. UC Berkeley interestingly places cellular and molecular biology into two separate departments, while other universities might combine them under one major discipline.

Many colleges and universities divide their programs into two basic categories based on what kind of system is studied: organismic biology and cellular biology. The main difference between these two categories is their primary level of focus. The whole organism is the center of interest with organismic biology, and cellular biology focuses more on what is happening at the cellular and molecular level within an organism.

How a university houses or groups its biology specialties, however, is not as important as the specialties it offers. To make sure you end up in the right program, do your research ahead of time. You can study college catalogs and make phone calls to department heads or advisors. Investigate the university's offerings and how those particular subject areas apply to the career path you are considering.

If you are not sure what area of biology you want to pursue as a career upon graduation, look for a university that offers a good general program, or one that has interdisciplinary studies that would allow you to cross over between subfields. Sometimes taking one particular course in an area, or being influenced by one dynamic professor, can help make the choice more evident to you. A program that allows you to experience a number of areas to help in your decision making would be the best bet.

Actually, with a general degree in biology, you could pursue most of the career paths covered in this book since specialization isn't required until the graduate level. But it is important to keep in mind that the career you might want to pursue could possibly require a master's or even a doctorate degree. The level of education you are willing to pursue will affect your career choice and as a result, the undergraduate program you decide to attend.

Most major colleges and universities can provide a good basic biology preparation, and for those who want to go on to graduate school, a general background is what is most sought after. Make sure to add math by way of calculus, some statistics, and some computer science to your curriculum. Your English, reading, and writing skills should be top-notch, too.

Selecting the right graduate school is more directed to specialization. You should not plan to study marine mammals at a school where no professors are involved in that specialty. You need to determine where the people are located who are involved in the area of concentration that interests you the most. By the time you have reached your last year of undergraduate study and you have done all the necessary groundwork, you should have a good idea of what you want to accomplish with graduate study.

## The Career Paths

What college student doesn't hope to find a great job upon graduation? With four years of study and careful planning throughout your college program, and for some fields a stint of graduate study, there is no reason why, as a biology major, you shouldn't walk into the plum job of your choosing.

There are a lot of choices, however, and the aim of this book is to help you narrow them down and find the career path that best suits your education, interests, and skills. For the purpose of this book, five main paths have been identified and explored, but they are in no way exhaustive. As you have already probably gleaned from reading the Introduction to this book, the list of main tracks numbers close to two dozen. Within those tracks are thousands of different job titles. Many are explored throughout the following five chapters, as primary paths or secondary and related paths; some are provided for you later in this chapter, under "Other Biology Career Paths" and "New Fields in Biology."

The five paths as outlined here are:

Path 1: Botanists
Path 2: Zoologists
Path 3: Aquatic scientists
Path 4: Medical scientists, technologists, and technicians
Path 5: Biology educators

As mentioned earlier, this list is by no means comprehensive. Many university programs allow for a great deal of latitude in designing majors and courses of study. It is now common practice to pursue interdisciplinary degrees. With a little bit of guidance and creativity, you should be able to make a case for your biology degree in any area you wish to enter.

## Other Biology Career Paths

In addition to the five major career paths mentioned previously, there are a few secondary paths of interest to the biology major. The following is a brief look at some of these related career paths.

### Agriculture
The world of agriculture, animal husbandry, food, and nutrition is a wide-open path for biology majors. It covers agronomy, which works to improve

the quality and production of field crops; animal science, which is an area that conducts research in selecting, breeding, feeding, managing, and marketing domesticated animals; food science, which involves the study of the chemical, physical, and biological nature of food to learn how to safely produce, preserve, package, distribute, and store it; and nutrition, which is concerned with counseling individuals or groups on sound nutritional practices to maintain and improve health.

Within this career path you will find job titles such as:

| | |
|---|---|
| Agricultural economist | Food and drug inspector |
| Agronomist | Food scientist |
| Brewmaster | Livestock scientist |
| Dairy manager/owner | Nutritionist |
| Farmer | Pest control specialist |

## Environmental Biology

In some universities environmental biology and ecology programs stand on their own; in others this discipline is considered a subfield of zoology.

Within this career path you will find job titles such as:

| | |
|---|---|
| Animal ecologist | Park ranger |
| Community ecologist | Plant ecologist |
| Conservation biologist | Pollution control technician |
| Ecological physiologist | Population ecologist |
| Environmental policy manager | Soil toxicologist |
| Evolutionary ecologist | Water engineer |
| Fisheries biologist | Watershed manager |
| Forest economist | Wildlife ecologist/manager (see a |
| Nature center curator | firsthand account for this job title |
| Paleontologist | in Chapter 7) |

## Information Systems

Categorizing and maintaining information and making it available to scholars, researchers, and the general public is an important aspect of biology work.

There are thousands of public, private, university, and hospital libraries that need professional librarians with a strong science background. Strong computer skills are also crucial.

Within this career path you will find job titles such as:

| | |
|---|---|
| Information systems specialist | Medical librarian |
| Library assistant | Science librarian |

## Science Writing, Illustration, and Photography

Science writers write about scientific and technical issues and often cover new discoveries or trends for newspapers, magazines, books, television, and radio. Some specialize in a particular topic, such as medicine or environmental issues, while others generalize and will write about any topic they know there's a market for. An important part of science writing is making technical information clear and understandable to the general public.

The work of scientific illustrators and photographers is used in medical textbooks and other publications, for research purposes, and in lectures and other presentations.

Within this career path you will find job titles such as:

| | |
|---|---|
| Biological illustrator | Medical illustrator |
| Biological photographer | Science writer |
| Media specialist | |

## Forensic Science

Forensic science is a catch-all phrase that includes any of the sciences as they are applied to litigation or adjudication, including chemistry, molecular biology, entomology, and toxicology.

Areas of study—and employment—include:

| | |
|---|---|
| Arson | Computer investigation |
| Chemistry | DNA |

*continued*

| | |
|---|---|
| Drugs | Linguistics and voice analysis |
| Engineering | Medicine |
| Fingerprints | Photography |
| Firearms | Shoe prints |
| Hair and fibers | Tire tracks |
| Handwriting | Toxicology |
| Image processing | Traffic accident investigation |

## New Fields in Biology

Two new fields in biology that are growing rapidly are biophysics and computer theoretical biology or computational biology, as it is also known.

Biophysics tends to have strong medical applications in x-rays, petscans, and MRI scans. Computer theoretical biology is, in part, an attempt to move away from using animals in research. Instead, computer models are used to explore evolution, development, and how a drug acts in a given cell system.

## For More Information

Researching the right career path to follow takes more than reading just one book. The more informed you are, the happier you will be with your career choice. At the end of each of the chapters that follow and in the Additional Resources section you will find scores of publications to investigate and professional associations to contact. Each will have something to offer you.

In addition, throughout the following chapters you will read firsthand accounts from people actually working in the various fields. They tell what each job really entails, what the duties are, what the lifestyle is like, what the upsides and downsides are. All of the professionals reveal what drew them to the field and how they got started. And so that you can make the best career decisions for yourself, each professional offers some expert advice based on years of personal experience.

But don't stop with these accounts. Find other professionals to talk to and follow around for a day or so. You can make contacts through your university's biology department or through the career guidance center. Nothing is more valuable than getting to see for yourself what a job is really like.

# 6

# Path I: Botanists

Botany is the study of plants. Plants have fascinated people for thousands of years. Without plants, we would not be able to breathe. Plants absorb carbon dioxide from the air and release life-sustaining oxygen. Without plants, we would not be able to eat. Our food—vegetables, fruit, meat, grains—is all derived, directly or indirectly, from plants.

Plants provide aesthetic beauty, enriching our homes and the environment. We depend upon plants for our clothing, shelter, fuel, the medicines that keep us healthy, the paper upon which these words are printed, and many other aspects of our existence.

To most people, the word *plant* means a range of living organisms from the smallest bacteria to the giant redwood and sequoia trees. With this definition in mind, plants include algae, fungi, lichens, mosses, ferns, conifers, and flowering plants. Modern scientists place bacteria, algae, and fungi into their own distinct kingdoms, but most general botany courses in most college and university botany departments still teach about these groups.

Botanists study plants and their environment. Some study all aspects of plant life; others specialize in areas such as identification and classification of plants, the structure and function of plant parts, the biochemistry of plant processes, the causes and cures of plant diseases, and the geological records of plants.

## Definition of the Career Path

In such a broad field, there are many kinds of botanists and many different career paths available.

Some botanists are called field botanists or field biologists and, with their strong interest in ecology, study the interactions of plants with other organisms and the environment. Some botanists working in the field study the structure of plants. They concentrate on the pattern of the whole plant. Other field botanists look for new species or conduct research and do experiments to discover how plants grow under different conditions.

There are botanists who conduct research and those who use the results to increase and improve our supply of food, medicines, fibers, building materials, and other plant products. For example, someone concerned about the world food supply can study plant pathology or plant breeding.

Conservationists with botanical knowledge and qualifications manage parks, forests, rangelands, and wilderness areas. Public health and environmental protection professionals use their botanical knowledge and understanding of plant science to help solve pollution problems.

Some botanists work in labs and use microscopes to study the detailed structure of individual cells. They perform experiments to discover how plants convert simple chemical compounds into more complex chemicals. They might study how genetic information in DNA controls plant development. Botanists also study the time scales of processes, ranging from fractions of a second in individual cells to those that take eons.

People with a mathematical background to couple with their knowledge of botany might pursue the fields of biophysics, developmental botany, genetics, modeling, or systems ecology. Those with an interest in chemistry can become plant physiologists, plant biochemists, molecular biologists (discussed in Chapter 9), or chemotaxonomists. Those intrigued by microscopic organisms can choose microbiology (examined in Chapter 9), phycology, or mycology.

Botanists who prefer to work with plants on an aesthetic level can enter into the fields of ornamental horticulture and landscape design. Those who enjoy working with people have a wide range of opportunities in teaching and public service, fields that are covered in more depth in Chapter 10.

As you can see, there are many specializations for biology majors and more specifically for those who wish to pursue botany. How the different paths are categorized varies from institution to institution and scientist to scientist but, in general, how universities combine or separate their departments often provides the easiest way to look at the different areas.

What follows are definitions of the different subdisciplines of botany:

### Plant Biology

- Anatomy studies microscopic plant structure—cells and tissues.

- Biochemistry covers the chemical aspects of plant life processes and includes the chemical products of plants (phytochemistry).
- Biophysics is the application of physics to plant life processes.
- Chemotaxonomy uses the chemicals produced by plants to aid in their identification.
- Cytology is the study of the structure, function, and life history of plant cells.
- Ecology studies the relationships between plants and their environments, both individually and in communities.
- Genetics investigates plant heredity and variation. Plant geneticists study genes and gene function in plants.
- Molecular biology studies the structure and function of biological macromolecules, including the biochemical and molecular aspects of genetics.
- Morphology studies macroscopic plant forms. It is also the study of evolution and development of leaves, roots, and stems.
- Paleobotany studies the biology and evolution of fossil plants.
- Physiology investigates the functions and vital processes of plants (and animals) under normal and abnormal conditions. Two examples of subjects studied by plant physiologists are photosynthesis and mineral nutrition.
- Systematics studies evolutionary history and relationships among plants.
- Systems ecology uses mathematical models to demonstrate concepts such as nutrient cycling.
- Taxonomy covers the identifying, naming, and classifying of plants.

**Applied Plant Sciences**
- Agronomy studies crop and soil sciences. Agronomists make practical use of plant and soil sciences to increase field crop yields.
- Biotechnology uses biological organisms in a number of ways: to produce useful products, improve crops, develop new drugs, or harness microbes to recycle wastes, to name just a few. Today many scientists narrow the definition even further and consider biotechnology to be the genetic modification of living organisms to produce useful products.
- Breeding involves the development of better types of plants, including selecting and crossing plants with desirable traits such as disease resistance.

- Economic botany covers plants with commercial importance. Economic botany also includes the study of harmful and beneficial plants and plant products.
- Food science and technology involves the development of food from various plant products.
- Forestry is managing forests for the production of timber and conservation.
- Horticulture covers the production of ornamental plants and fruit and vegetable crops. Landscape design is also an important subdiscipline in horticulture.
- Natural resource management is the responsible use and protection of our natural resources for the benefit of all.
- Plant pathology studies plant diseases, both the biological aspects of disease and disease management or control.

**Organismal Specialties**
- Bryology is the study of mosses and similar plants, covering all aspects of these plants, including their identification, classification, and ecology.
- Lichenology is the study of lichens, dual organisms that are composed of both a fungus and an alga.
- Microbiology is the study of microorganisms. Microbiologists may be grouped by the organism they study, such as bacteria, or by the branch of biology, such as microbial ecology.
- Mycology is the study of fungi. Fungi have a tremendous impact on our world and are important in the biosphere because they help recycle dead organic material. Some fungi are important producers of biological products such as vitamins and antibiotics.
- Phycology is the study of algae, the base of the food chain in aquatic environments. Phycologists who study algae in oceans are sometimes called marine biologists, covered in Chapter 8.
- Pteridology is the study of ferns and similar plants.

**Botany Education**
- Botany educators provide knowledge and insight about plants, plant biology, and the ecological roles of plants. This specialty includes teaching in schools, museums, and botanical gardens, development of educational materials, and science writing.

## Possible Job Titles

For every "ology" there's an "ist," an "er," and more. Here is a sample of possible job titles for botanists:

| | |
|---|---|
| Arborist | Lichenologist |
| Bryologist | Morphologist |
| Chemotaxonomist | Natural resources manager |
| Curator | Paleobotanist |
| Ecologist | System ecologist |
| Forest economist | Topiary trainer |
| Golf course manager | Tree surgeon |
| Horticultural therapist | Wood technologist |
| Interiorscaper | |

## Possible Employers

The major employers of plant biologists are educational institutions, federal and state agencies, industries, and botanical gardens.

Educational institutions, which employ the majority of botanists, range from high schools and community colleges to universities. Although high schools and community colleges have relatively few openings for those wanting to teach specialized courses—and there is little time or equipment for research activity—botanists who enjoy working with people and sharing their knowledge can find these positions satisfying.

Most positions for professional plant scientists are in colleges and universities. Almost all colleges and universities offer courses in the various disciplines of botany and plant science, and botanists with different specialities can be successful at finding faculty positions. Educational institutions also employ botanists as researchers and as administrators.

Government agencies on both the federal and state levels employ botanists in many different fields. Plant biologists work in various branches of the U.S. Department of Agriculture, including the Medical Plant Resources Laboratory, the Germplasm Resources Laboratory, the Animal and Plant Health Inspection Service, the National Arboretum, and the U.S. Forest Service.

The U.S. Department of the Interior—which includes the National Park Service, the Bureau of Land Management, and the U.S. Geological Survey—also employs botanists. Plant scientists work in several other federal agencies as well, including the Public Health Service, State Department, National Aeronautics and Space Administration, Smithsonian Institution, and the Environmental Protection Agency.

Each of the fifty state governments also employs plant scientists in agencies parallel to those of the federal government. Environmental organizations, such as the Nature Conservancy, also hire botanists.

Industry is the third largest employer of botanists. The oil and chemical industries, drug companies, lumber and paper companies, seed and nursery companies, fruit growers, food companies, fermentation industries (including breweries), biological supply houses, and biotechnology firms all hire trained botanists.

Botanical gardens and arboreta (the plural of *arboretum*) also provide jobs for botanists. Botanical gardens and arboreta are parks open to the general public, students, and research scientists. Plants, flowers, trees, and shrubs are collected from all over the world and exhibited in arrangements by family, country of origin, or with regard to aesthetics.

Typical visitors to botanical gardens and arboreta generally fall into six categories: dedicated professional scientists and horticulturalists who utilize the gardens' collections for research purposes or to identify specific plants; professional and amateur gardeners who participate in adult education classes and training programs; horticultural students enrolled in internship programs through their universities; local residents who come to enjoy a peaceful sanctuary; schoolchildren and their teachers; and international travelers and scientists interested in the collections and history of the gardens. Given the diversity of visitors to a botanical garden, one can see the possibilities for various types of employment in this setting. From specialists who conduct research and maintain the collections, to teachers who instruct students and lead training programs, to guides knowledgeable about the history and the collections, there are many opportunities for botanists to work in such an environment.

Of the potential employers of botanists, botanical gardens are perhaps the most familiar to the public. For this reason, we will spend some time discussing their importance, as well as some of the various positions available to biology majors at gardens and arboreta.

Public botanical gardens and arboreta play an important role in horticultural education. Through the design, interpretation, and management of a variety of collections of plants, trees, and shrubs, botanical gardens and arboreta perform the following functions:

- **Public programs.** Botanical gardens and arboreta generally offer public programs such as classes in gardening, question-and-answer hotlines to help with gardening problems, tours of the grounds, and lectures on the various collections. These programs help to teach people how to care for their plants, add to their knowledge of unusual or new plants, and help foster an understanding of and appreciation for landscape design.
- **Research.** Most botanical gardens and arboreta are involved with ongoing research issues. Curators and other horticulturists go on collection trips to add to the types of plants in their gardens and to study the plant life in other geographic regions. Living plants are added to the grounds and pressed and dried plants are stored in herbaria and are shared with researchers all over the world. Through these activities, garden professionals are able to save rare and endangered plants by studying their requirements and offering a protected environment while reintroducing them to the wild.
- **Introduction of new plants.** Public gardens play a role in introducing new plants to the nursery and home landscaping markets through plant collecting, selection, and breeding.
- **Beautification.** Public gardens provide a tranquil setting in the midst of busy cities for walkers and nature lovers.
- **Preservation.** Historic gardens are preserved and interpreted to the public through the use of slides, films, lectures, brochures, and labels.
- **Conservation education.** Public gardens help both children and adults to develop an appreciation for gardening and a concern about protecting the natural environment.
- **Community improvement.** Public gardens participate in city beautification projects through education, plant breeding, and selection.

Plant biologists and biology majors with an interest in botany or training in related disciplines also find work in nurseries and floral shops, landscape architecture and design firms, and with the Cooperative Extension Service, which tries to bring university research into the community.

Botany offers a range of interesting and worthwhile career opportunities. The work is frequently varied and the surroundings usually pleasant. Because of the diversity in the plant sciences, people with many different educational backgrounds, skills, and interests can find a satisfying career in botany.

## Training and Qualifications

A bachelor's degree is the usual minimum requirement for most careers in botany. With a bachelor's degree, graduates can find positions as laboratory technicians or technical assistants in education, industry, government, museums, parks, and botanical gardens.

As is true in many other fields, the more education you have, the wider the range of positions that are open to you. Many positions require a master's or doctorate. A Ph.D. is required for most teaching and research positions in colleges and universities.

The courses you select in your undergraduate program will vary depending on the curriculum of the college you attend and your own interests. To be best prepared for the job market, you should get a broad general education in language, arts, humanities, and the social sciences in addition to specializing in plant biology. Most positions require good oral and written skills and computer abilities, too.

Most botany programs require courses in math and statistics, as well as chemistry and physics. For those hoping to work abroad, foreign language expertise is also desirable. Many colleges and universities require a core program in biology before you can enroll in specialized botany courses. At other institutions you are allowed to take botany courses right away.

## Career Outlook

Plant science is an expanding field that includes agronomy, crop science, entomology, and plant breeding. This is becoming a very popular field as more and more people recognize the importance of plants to many different aspects of society.

Expected ongoing research in biotechnology will result in job opportunities for food scientists and technicians as our need for improved food supplies continues to grow. Increasing concerns about pollution and the need to protect our air and water supplies will lead to more jobs for ecologists in government and industry. The search for new drugs and medicines and useful genes for improving crop supplies will continue to create a need for botanical researchers. Anticipated growth in landscape ecology and the preservation and restoration of wetlands will lead to employment gains in landscape architecture and ecology. Additional positions will become available as current workers retire or otherwise leave the profession, especially in academia.

However, the federal government funds much research and development. Recent budget tightening has led to smaller increases in research and development expenditures, further limiting the dollar amount of each grant. The number of grants awarded, though, has remained fairly constant.

A degree in botany can provide the foundation for employment in several important and rewarding careers in biology.

## Earnings

According to the National Association of Colleges and Employers, beginning salary offers in private industry in 2000 averaged $29,235 a year for bachelor's degree recipients in biological science, about $35,667 for master's degree recipients, and about $42,744 for doctoral degree recipients. Median annual earnings for biological and life scientists were about $49,239 in 2000.

In the federal government in 2001, general biological scientists in nonsupervisory, supervisory, and managerial positions earned an average salary of $61,236; microbiologists averaged $67,835; ecologists $61,936; physiologists $78,366; and geneticists $72,510.

Salaries always depend on experience and education. In addition, the geographic location of the employer also makes a difference. In general, salaries vary with the cost of living in any particular region.

The sense of accomplishment and satisfaction that comes from doing interesting and worthwhile work is one of the rewards of a career in plant science. In addition, many positions in botany provide other benefits such as individual freedom, varied work, pleasant surroundings, stimulating associates, and the opportunity to travel.

## Close-Ups

With a degree as far-reaching as biology and a specialty in botany encompassing so many fields, it's impossible to give a full look at each one in the scope of just one book. However, to give you a taste of selected careers that would appeal to some botany majors, read the following descriptions of current positions in the field. You'll find other similar accounts from people in related fields in the chapters to come. What better way to learn about a career than from a person working in the field?

Consider the job of Susan Kelley, curatorial associate for the living collection at Arnold Arboretum in Jamaica Plain, Massachusetts. The arboretum is affiliated with Harvard University, and its mission is the biology, cultivation, and conservation of temperate woody plants. Susan's job involves mapping the living specimens on the grounds and labeling each plant.

Susan describes the arboretum as "more than a horticultural garden. Our collections are used scientifically . . . visitors from all over the world use our collections for study." Within this scientific environment, her duties include maintaining maps of each collection, adding each year's one thousand new plantings to maps, field checking each specimen's condition, and labeling every plant.

Susan's record-keeping begins when a plant goes from the nursery to the grounds. She works closely with her boss, the horticultural taxonomist, who determines what will be planted every spring and fall. Susan is responsible for mapping the new plantings. In addition, she has also been responsible for transcribing the arboretum's hand-drawn maps of collections to computerized maps.

Another of Susan's responsibilities is the coordination of volunteers and summer interns. This involves training and managing personnel, which is time consuming. Adding to the difficulty is the fact that applicants for the intern program come from around the world; Susan must interview these applicants by telephone and make acceptance decisions without personal interviews.

Most of Susan's time is spent outdoors, regardless of the season. Winter provides the opportunity to field check the conifer collection and to more easily see labels on many plants. This is balanced by some computer work that she finds challenging as well.

Susan Kelley earned both a bachelor's and master's degree in music before deciding to pursue a career in botany. She received a master's degree in plant population ecology from City University of New York and initially worked at the Harvard University Herbaria before applying for her present position.

Another interesting job is that of Rick Darke, curator of plants at Longwood Gardens in Kennett Square, Pennsylvania. Longwood Gardens is primarily a display garden. Unlike a traditional botanic garden, the collections at Longwood are used more as part of the landscape. As Rick describes it, "We have a lot more emphasis on the art of the landscape, the pleasure derived by people being in that landscape, than we have people coming to study these plants as objects."

In addition to overseeing the identification, labeling, and mapping done by curatorial assistants like Susan Kelley, Rick's responsibilities include serving on landscape and advisory committees to recommend new plants and comment on architectural details, and extensive teaching (botany for Professional Gardener students, other graduate student courses, and a continuing education program that includes evening lectures and field trips). This interaction with students, in combination with his other responsibilities, is what Rick likes most about his work: "We usually have an intern in the office, and I'm constantly teaching people as they move through the organization. Over the years you can imagine the wonderful network you make of friends and professional colleagues around the country and around the world."

Rick also writes for an in-house publication and for magazines. For example, he wrote an article about a garden created for Longwood by a landscape architect Rick met in Brazil and brought back to Pennsylvania for the project. He has traveled extensively to look for new plants for Longwood Gardens, visiting Australia, New Zealand, Japan, South Africa, Brazil, England, and Germany. He is a member of the Garden Writers Association of America and is the author of *For Your Garden: Ornamental Grasses* (published by Little, Brown).

Rick Darke has a bachelor's degree in plant sciences from the University of Delaware. He began as an intern at Longwood Gardens and later became an assistant taxonomist. He took some graduate courses in plant systematics and taxonomy, but in Rick's case, an advanced degree was not necessary to attain his current position. He was given the opportunity to assume a Ph.D. position that was rewritten as a curator of plants. In Rick's words, "The man I was working for was due to retire in two years, and it was a question of would I learn more by staying on the job and developing the skills I'd need to take over, or would I learn more by getting into a graduate program. My choice to stay worked out."

---

### ADVICE FROM THE PROFESSIONALS

Susan Kelley discusses career options for mappers and labelers:

"This is a great job; I could feasibly stay here for a long time. There's so much more to learn. For example, there's another mapping system I'm interested in—GIS, Geographic Information System.

"With more experience, more study and research, and publications, one could move up into a curatorial position. I'd want to become more proficient with taxonomic work and go on collecting trips. We have a research program in Indonesia, and I'd love to go there one day and do mapping at their botanical gardens."

Rick Darke suggests that the following skills, in addition to a love of plants, are necessary for success in his profession:

"You need good writing skills and verbal communication. I could not do what I do, and I would not have had the opportunities, if I hadn't worked on being able to articulate my notions."

## Strategies for Finding the Jobs

In any type of career pursuit, coupling hands-on training with your theoretical program is highly desirable. If possible, arrange to do fieldwork or an undergraduate research project under one of your professors. The project might include helping the professor with research or pursuing your own interests. The experience will help you decide the area or areas of botany you like best—or might want to avoid. Research experience will also be very helpful should you decide to pursue graduate work.

In addition, internships, work-study programs, cooperative education, or summer jobs can provide important additional experience. Students who establish themselves during one of these programs often find they have a foot firmly planted in the door once graduation comes and they are looking for full-time employment. These positions occur in government agencies, college and university research laboratories, botanical gardens and arboreta, agricultural experiment stations, freshwater and marine biological stations, and within private industries.

The more experience you can add to your résumé while you're still studying, the more employable you'll be. Don't forget your faculty members and advisors as a great source of leads and contacts. Networking really does work.

Contact the following professional associations for more information about careers in botany. Many publish books, pamphlets, and brochures with career information, as well as newsletters and journals that list job openings.

## Professional Associations

**American Institute of Biological Sciences**
1444 Eye St. NW, Suite 200
Washington, DC 20005
aibs.org

**American Physiological Society**
9650 Rockville Pike
Bethesda, MD 20814-3991
the-aps.org

**American Phytopathological Society**
3340 Pilot Knob Rd.
St. Paul, MN 55121-2097
apsnet.org

**American Society for Horticultural Science**
113 S. West St., Suite 200
Alexandria, VA 22314-2851
E-mail: webmaster@ashs.org
ashs.org

**American Society of Agronomy**
677 S. Segoe Rd.
Madison, WI 53711
E-mail: headquarters@agronomy.org
agronomy.org

**American Society of Plant Biologists**
15501 Monona Dr.
Rockville, MD 20855
E-mail: info@aspb.org
aspb.org

**American Society of Plant Taxonomists**
Department of Botany
University of Wyoming
Laramie, WY 82071-3165
sysbot.org

**Botanical Society of America**
Business Manager
P.O. Box 299
St. Louis, MO 63166-0299
E-mail: bsa-manager@botany.org
botany.org

**Ecological Society of America**
1707 H St. NW, Suite 400
Washington, DC 20006
E-mail: esahq@esa.org
esa.org

**Mycological Society of America and Phycological Society of America**
P.O. Box 1897
Lawrence, KS 66044-8897
msafungi.org

**Palentology Research Institute**
1259 Trumansberg Rd.
Ithaca, NY 14850

**Society of American Foresters**
5400 Grosvenor Lane
Bethesda, MD 20814-2198
E-mail: safnet@safnet.org
safnet.org

# 7

# Path 2: Zoologists

For some the term *zoology* conjures up images of bespectacled gentlemen peering through microscopes or gutsy women out in the wild communing with chimpanzees or gorillas. The reality is that zoology is a broad field that defies stereotypes and offers many career choices.

A counterpart to botany, zoology is the discipline of biology that studies animals, including birds, insects, reptiles, fish, invertebrates, mammals, and microscopic organisms. Zoology covers physiology on a microscopic level, development throughout an animal's life span, the interaction of animals with their environments, and how things have changed over long periods of time. Zoologists study both land and marine animal life at all levels of organization: ecosystem, community, population, whole organism, cellular, and molecular.

Just as with botany, which was covered in the previous chapter, knowledge of biological principles related to zoology is central to the well-being of mankind, particularly at a time when increasing populations and the accompanying strain are hurting our planet's ecosystems. There is also a new awareness of the need to solve health and social problems. Many zoologists are also addressing humane and ethical issues.

## Definition of the Career Path

Zoology is a discipline that offers a broad choice of career paths. Your degree can serve you well in a number of settings, from industry to health care. In short, you can find zoologists employed in the obvious as well as most unexpected places.

Zoology can be viewed as a basic science or an applied one. As a basic science, the zoologist satisfies his or her curiosity about living things but does not consider whether the information gained is immediately useful. Applied or field scientists use their knowledge for the betterment of mankind and animal life.

Zoology can be broadly grouped into the following categories:

Applied zoology includes wildlife management, environmental protection, agriculture, fisheries, aquaculture, and public education programs such as those found in zoos and aquariums.

Behavior experts study animal behavior for a number of purposes including handling, training, and research.

Ecology studies the interactions of animals with other organisms and the environment.

Evolution and systematics study evolutionary history and relationships among animals.

Molecular biology (as related to zoology) and genetics study the structure and function of biological macromolecules, including the biochemical and molecular aspects of genetics.

Morphology studies macroscopic animal forms.

Paleontology studies the fossil remains of animals (and plants). Scientists trace the evolution and development of past life and use fossils to reconstruct prehistoric environments and geography. They also make models of animals that have become extinct, such as dinosaurs.

Physiology investigates the functions and vital processes of animals.

Systematics or taxonomy is the identification and study of the kinds of organisms of the past and living today, and of the relationships among these organisms.

## Possible Job Titles

Because of the varied job settings, the job titles a zoology major can hold are equally varied. There is often overlap, too, between the different job settings. You can find a curator, for example, working in a natural history museum or in a zoo or marine park.

Here is a sampling of some of the most common job titles. Your own research will probably allow you to add to the list:

| | |
|---|---|
| Animal behavior consultant | Conservation officer |
| Animal physiologist | Curator |

*continued*

| | |
|---|---|
| Entomologist | Nature center director |
| Environmental impact analyst | Ornithologist |
| Fisheries biologist | Parasitologist |
| Game manager | Systematic biologist |
| Herpetologist | Taxidermist |
| Ichthyologist | Trainer |
| Life sciences technician | Wildlife biologist |
| Mammalogist | Zookeeper |

## Possible Job Settings

A degree in zoology can lead to a career in a number of interesting fields. Here is a look at a few possible employers for the zoology major.

### Education
This sector is probably the largest employer of graduates with a degree in biology. Opportunities in schools, colleges, and universities are discussed in Chapter 10.

### Health Care
A degree in biology and specifically in zoology can be the stepping-stone for work as a medical clinician, scientist, or technician. Opportunities in the medical field are covered in depth in Chapter 9.

### Government
Although many positions in government involve policymaking and regulation, other government scientists are engaged in basic and applied research. The Bureau of Land Management, Bureau of Indian Affairs, Bureau of Reclamation, U.S. Forestry Service, U.S. Fish and Wildlife Service, U.S. Army Corps of Engineers, U.S. Department of Agriculture, Department of Defense, U.S. Food and Drug Administration, Department of Environmental Protection and Energy, National Park Service, and the Department of the Interior are just a few of the federal agencies that employ zoologists.

### Industry
Most zoologists with positions in industry are likely to be involved in research and product development. However, many jobs in industry and commerce do not necessarily involve the direct application of knowledge gained from

a zoology degree. Employers prefer applicants with university degrees and utilize their talents in sales and management positions.

## Information and Arts

There is a wide spectrum of jobs in publishing, broadcasting, and filmmaking for zoology majors. With the general public's increased interest in current science and technology issues, particularly those related to the environment, conservation, and health, there is a large market for nature-related programs, books, and articles.

Newspapers and magazines run regular features and need writers with scientific backgrounds to translate their knowledge into language that is easily understood by the general public. Publishers of professional journals also need biologists for in-house editing, and publishers of textbooks might require biological illustrators.

Many industries require skilled writers to produce technical documents describing their products and their proper use. A bachelor's degree is usually adequate for these types of positions but additional training in communications, journalism, or broadcasting, as well as demonstrated writing skill, is often required.

## Museums, Zoos, and Aquariums

For many field zoologists, museums, zoos, and aquariums are the natural choice for a career setting and offer many different kinds of positions for those with a zoology degree. Positions involve research, working directly with the animals, administration, and public education.

Although aquatic science is an area of zoology, it is such a large—and popular—field that it can be considered a separate career path and, thus, has been given the attention it deserves in its own chapter, Chapter 8.

# Training and Qualifications

From the beginning of your degree program you should be aware that your academic record will follow you wherever you go. You will be competing with other new graduates, and in addition to personal references and hands-on training earned through internships or work-study positions, your grade point average will be another criterion used to judge you.

Getting ahead in your chosen career can also be closely linked to your academic performance. For example, a scholarship might be necessary to pursue a master's or doctorate degree or you may need to take an expensive course that has a fee-waiver for students with the strongest needs and the best records.

In addition to your academic record, you will need to acquire practical experience as soon as possible during your undergraduate years. Most university departments and many government agencies and private industries provide summer job opportunities or academic-year internships, co-op jobs, or work-study programs for research assistants or other entry-level positions. These positions will not only provide you with the training you need, they will also help you make valuable contacts that will be useful for obtaining permanent career positions after your formal education has been completed.

Communication and computer skills are also crucial to getting ahead in this field. Concise writing and the ability to make oral presentations are part of most jobs. Computer literacy is a skill most employers require of their new hires. The ability to learn computer programs specific to one's job, as well as being able to use basic software to prepare reports and to communicate effectively through E-mail are now fundamental parts of most jobs.

When choosing your training program, remember also that those with combined degrees will fare best in certain fields. For example, a B.S.-level zoologist who goes on to earn a law degree can work in environmental law, and a zoologist with a communications minor can work as a scientific writer or illustrator.

## Career Outlook

The overall employment outlook for biological scientists through 2010 is for faster than average job growth. Zoologists study the origin, behavior, diseases, and life processes of animals; much of this research can lead to advances in human health care and the betterment of our environment. However, recent budget cutbacks have led to smaller increases in federal research and development expenditures, limiting the amount of money awarded to each grant.

In the many areas of possible employment for zoologists mentioned earlier, competition should be expected for the most sought-after jobs. With zoology careers, just like in any other profession, the best-trained and most experienced applicants will get the best jobs.

## Earnings

Salaries for zoologists differ greatly, depending upon the setting, type of job, and experience. Zoologists do not enter their profession for the love of money. Although wages can be considered small compared to other more high-profile careers, zoologists over time can advance up the pay scale and earn a comfortable living.

As discussed earlier in this chapter, government employees are subject to the government pay scale. Those working in educational settings earn the same as other educators in different fields. Consultants can charge a flat hourly fee for their work.

Zookeepers often begin at the bottom of the salary scale, usually in the high teens or low twenties. As they move up the ranks to positions of increasing responsibility, their salaries move up too. Curators earn anywhere between $30,000 to $55,000 or $60,000, depending upon the facility's budget and the amount of experience and seniority they have amassed.

Those working in research and development or sales for private industry can expect to earn the highest salaries. Those who move up the administrative ladder in almost any setting also increase their earnings. But as mentioned earlier, the more administrative the job, the less hands-on work is involved. And hands-on work was often the original attraction to the field.

## Close-Ups

A concentration in zoology can prepare you for any number of career possibilities. Let's look at some different jobs through the eyes of the professionals working in the field.

Carin Peterson is animal curator at the Austin Zoo in Austin, Texas. She has a B.A. in zoology and is pursuing a master's degree in wildlife biology, and has attended seminars and participated in veterinary technician training. Carin has been working in the field since 1992.

Carin answered an ad for an animal caretaker and was hired immediately after her interview. The job allowed her to combine her interests in research, science, nature, and animals. She began as a zookeeper and worked up to animal department supervisor.

The daily responsibilities of an animal curator vary according to what needs to be done. Carin's basic job description includes maintaining animal records, coordinating veterinary care and visits, advising on diets and husbandry, consulting on acquisitions and departures, and supervising and training the keeper staff. She also answers E-mail, maintains a web page, and is involved with basic animal training.

Carin Peterson feels that her job is always interesting, and she especially enjoys the ongoing opportunity to learn more about animals. She usually works a forty-hour week but often works additional hours to help out the staff. As Carin says, "Usually my day is pretty relaxed, but that can change in an instant. There can be a lot of stress involved, especially if there is a complicated veterinary procedure to be done or an animal is sick or very pregnant, if the weather is bad, or if there are deadlines to be met—just like anywhere else."

As mentioned earlier, a major in zoology can pave the way for a wide variety of careers. Leon Fager worked for the U.S. Forest Service for thirty-one years as Threatened and Endangered Species Program manager. He combined his B.S. in wildlife management with a master's degree in forestry to pursue a career that met his interest in wildlife and wetlands. He has worked in Arizona, Nevada, South Dakota, Michigan, Colorado, and New Mexico.

Living near three national wildlife refuges allowed Leon to become familiar with the management of habitat for waterfowl and desert bighorn sheep; this led to his commitment to the profession: "The work appealed to me because with most wildlife and fish habitat improvement projects you can see immediate results, the wildlife or fish benefiting from my work. I enjoyed being part of a national effort to improve conditions for wildlife on our public lands."

An entry-level biologist working in a government agency must learn how the agency functions and how to implement its mission. Leon initially worked with foresters, range conservationists, soil scientists, and engineers to learn how their various jobs fit together. He helped foresters design timber sites to provide shelter and food for wildlife, and developed water for wildlife in these areas.

Under the Endangered Species Act, the U.S. Forest Service is responsible for protecting habitat for all federally listed wildlife species. This means that the agency must ascertain that its management activities do not destroy nesting areas; the biologist must survey large areas to check for the presence of any rare species. The biologist then prepares a report on the possible impact of the project on wildlife; the report is sent to the U.S. Fish and Wildlife Service for review.

As his career progressed, Leon Fager spent less time in the field and more time performing administrative duties such as formulating the budget and preparing litigation reports on lawsuits involving alleged violations of the Endangered Species Act. He also worked closely with other agencies, such as the U.S. Fish and Wildlife Service, and conservation organizations that provided money to the Forest Service for habitat improvement projects. Leon would design the project, oversee the construction, and report to the conservation organization. Some examples of these projects are wildlife water development, wetland development, and stream improvement.

Some areas of zoology allow great flexibility. According to Leon Fager, however, "Working for a federal agency is a very structured experience. I was required to be at work at a given time, keep a time sheet, and follow regulations. Performance is measured more by the ability to follow the rules and being loyal to the Forest Service than creativity and production." Employees of the U.S. Forest Service are compensated according to the pay schedule established by the Civil Service Commission. This is a tightly structured scale in which jobs are classified by complexity and required skills.

Pursuing an advanced degree and combining biology with other disciplines can lead to a wide range of career possibilities. Dr. Mary Lee Nitschke, animal behaviorist, has a Ph.D. in comparative developmental psychology from Michigan State University. She has forty years' experience in behavior modification and research, and is also a trainer and consultant. In addition, Dr. Nitschke is a tenured, full professor in the psychology department at Linfield College in Portland, Oregon, and co-owner of Animal School Pet Behavior Services.

Dr. Nitschke grew up in Texas, where "my major entertainment and stimulation came from observing animals." She trained horses before college and as an undergraduate worked in a kennel that bred and trained collies. In college, this interest in animal behavior combined with an interest in machines and engineering psychology. Dr. Nitschke began to see a connection between animal training and the psychology and learning theory she was studying.

Graduate school presented the opportunity to integrate these two interests. Dr. Nitschke's graduate studies targeted the "interspecies communication of distress"; she studied bobwhite quail, jackrabbits, coyotes, blue jays, and human babies to look for the existence of "some universality of understanding of the distress call between species."

Through Animal School Pet Behavior Services, Dr. Nitschke assists clients with pet behavior problems. For example, she consulted with a client whose dog had bitten several people. Dr. Nitschke evaluated the situation, studying the animal and analyzing the circumstances surrounding each of the biting incidents. She then presented the pet owner with some possible options and solutions.

Dr. Nitschke also does a considerable amount of public speaking and is a consultant for the invisible-fencing industry. She also trains animal control workers in how to approach and pick up unfamiliar animals. In addition, she teaches animal training and animal assisted therapy.

Dr. Mary Lee Nitschke's career is an example of how an interest in zoology, combined with additional education and training, can lead to diverse and fascinating opportunities for biology majors.

## ADVICE FROM THE PROFESSIONALS

For those interested in working in zoos, Carin Peterson offers this advice:

"Education and experience are both important. Most zoos today want at least two years of college focusing on classes in the natural sciences. If you can't get paid experience, volunteer or intern if possible. Working anywhere with animals is helpful, but exotics have special needs, so experience with them is a plus. Be well-rounded. Zoo employees need skills such as working with and talking to the public, computer literacy, time management, and handling basic tools—not just animal experience. Also, join professional organizations such as the American Association of Zookeepers or the American Zoo and Aquarium Association to know what is happening in the field."

Leon Fager's long career with the U.S. Forest Service gives him this perspective:

"In college I think it would be very valuable to take as many political science, communications, and social science courses as possible. Students like to take the biology courses because that's what they're interested in, but when you get into the job you soon find that politics and your ability to effectively communicate is just as, and maybe more, important than the biology.

"After graduation, my advice is to find work either with a state wildlife agency or a private contractor. State agencies work with animals and are generally less structured than the Forest Service. The opportunity to be in the field is much greater. There are an increasing number of private contractors who do surveys, reports, and projects for the Forest Service. I suggest that this would be a good place to work without having to conform to the rules and regulations of the Forest Service."

Dr. Mary Lee Nitschke has the following suggestions for those interested in working as animal behaviorists:

"For someone who wants to become an animal behaviorist, first of all, you have to have hands-on experience. And the more time you spend observing animals and learning how to interact with them, the better off you're going to be. The second thing is that you have to get educated to learn to understand, evaluate, and think like a scientist.

"Hands-on experience is very important. I don't think this is a profession that can be done totally by theory. On the other hand, the hands-on experience can't come totally from trial-and-error methods.

"I think the best route is to take a lot of experimental courses—psychology or in other fields. Some anthropology courses do a good job of preparing

*continued*

people. There are disciplines of animal behavior both within psychology and zoology. I think that a good psychology background is important, not just for experimental psych, but if you take a major in psychology in almost any school in the country, you will have to take experimental psychology and statistics."

## Strategies for Finding the Jobs

Hit the library! There are directories galore that list professional associations, zoos, universities, and corporations by industry. Make friends with your reference librarian and bring plenty of change for the copy machine. In addition, many of the professional associations listed at the end of this chapter post job listings and offer helpful links and information.

## Professional Associations

The following list of associations can be used as a valuable resource guide in locating additional information about specific careers. Many of the organizations publish newsletters listing job and internship opportunities, and still others offer an employment service to members. A quick look at the organizations' names will give you an idea of how large the scope is.

General information about education and careers in science in the United States may be obtained from:

**National Science**
  **Foundation**
4201 Wilson Blvd.
Arlington, VA 22230
nsf.gov

**The Society for Integrative**
  **and Comparative Biology**
1313 Dolly Madison Blvd., Suite 402
McLean, VA 22101
E-mail: sicb@BurkInc.com
sicb.org

**Animal Behavior**
American Society of
    Animal Science
1111 N. Dunlap Ave.
Savoy, IL 61874
E-mail: asas@assochq.org
asas.org

**Animal School Pet
    Behavior Services**
2364 NW Northrup
Portland, OR 97210
animalschoolservices.com

**Association for the Study of
    Animal Behaviour**
ASAB Membership Secretary
82A High St.
Sawston, Cambridge CB2 4HJ
United Kingdom
societies.ncl.ac.uk

**EATM (Exotic Animal
    Training and
    Management)**
Moorpark College
7075 Campus Rd.
Moorpark, CA 93021
http://sunny.moorparkcollege.edu
(A two-year training program.)

**IMATA (International Marine
    Animal Trainers
    Association)**
1200 S. Lake Shore Dr.
Chicago, IL 60605
http://tstr.saic.com/IMATA/home.asp
This organization can provide you with a list of recognized training
    programs.

**The Latham Foundation for the Promotion of Humane Education**
"Promoting respect for all life through education."
Latham Plaza Building
1826 Clement Ave.
Alameda, CA 95401
E-mail: info@latham.org
latham.org

## Animal Caretaking

For information on animal caretaking and the animal shelter and control personnel training program, write to:

**Animal Caretakers Information**
The Humane Society of the United States
2100 L Street NW, Suite 100
Washington, DC 20037
hsus.org

For information on training and certification of kennel staff and owners, contact:

**American Boarding Kennel Association**
1702 E. Pikes Ave.
Colorado Springs, CO 80909
abka.com

## Conservation, Wildlife, and Rehabilitation

The National Wildlife Rehabilitators Association is an organization for people interested in and concerned about the welfare of wildlife. Structured mainly for active rehabilitators, NWRA membership also includes professional wildlife personnel, conservationists, educators, naturalists, researchers, veterinarians, people from zoos and humane societies, and many others interested in improving knowledge of wild animals and ensuring their survival. The NWRA is incorporated solely for the support of the science and profession of wildlife rehabilitation and its practitioners.

For more information and to become a member, contact:

**National Wildlife Rehabilitators Association**
Central Office
14 N. 7th Ave.
St. Cloud, MN 56303-4766
nwrawildlife.org

The International Wildlife Rehabilitation Council (IWRC) is a professional organization for wildlife rehabilitators, founded to develop and disseminate information on the rehabilitation and care of wild animals, with the goal of returning them to their native environment.

For more information and to become a member, contact:

**International Wildlife Rehabilitation Council**
829 Bancroft Way
Berkeley, CA 94710
E-mail: iwrc@iwrc-online.org
iwrc-online.org

For information from other sources, contact:

**American Institute of Biological Sciences**
1444 Eye Street NW, Suite 200
Washington, DC 20005
aibs.org

**Department of Environmental Protection**
   **and Energy**
Division of Fish and Wildlife
P.O. Box 400
Trenton, NJ 08625-0400
state.nj.us/dep/fgw

**National Wildlife Federation**
11100 Wildlife Center Dr.
Reston, VA 20190-5362
nwf.org

**Student Conservation Association**
Resource Assistant Program
689 River Rd.
Charlestown, NH 03603-0550
thesca.org

**U.S. Fish and Wildlife Service**
Volunteer Program
1011 E. Tudor Rd.
Anchorage, AK 99503-6199
generalinfo.fws.gov

**U.S. Office of Personnel Management**
Visit opm.gov for information on job opportunities for students and
summer jobs in the federal government.

## Veterinary Medicine and Veterinary Technology
For information on careers in veterinary medicine and veterinary technology, contact:

**American Association of Zoo Veterinarians**
Executive Director
6 N. Pennell Rd.
Media, PA 19063
http://aazv.org

**American Veterinary**
**Medical Association**
1931 N. Meacham Rd., Suite 100
Schaumburg, IL 60173-4360
E-mail: avmainfo@avma.org
avma.org

For information on veterinary education, contact:

**Association of American Veterinary**
**Medical Colleges**
1101 Vermont Ave. NW, Suite 710
Washington, DC 20005
aavmc.org

For information on scholarships, grants, and loans, contact the financial
aid office at the veterinary schools to which you wish to apply.

## Zoo and Aquarium Associations
Zoo associations have been formed in many different countries. The largest
is the American Association of Zoological Parks and Aquariums, founded in
1924. Other zoo federations include those of Great Britain and Ireland, Spain
and Spanish America, Japan, Poland, and Germany.

The following organizations disseminate information on zoo management, exchange of specimens, and conservation of wildlife.

**American Association of Zookeepers**
Metro Washington Park Zoo
4001 SW Canyon Rd.
Portland, OR 97221
aazk.org

**American Zoo and Aquarium Association**
8403 Colesville Rd., Suite 710
Silver Spring, MD 20910-3314
aza.org

**Association of Zoo and Aquarium Docents**
E-mail: webmaster@azadocents.org
azadocents.org
(For volunteering opportunities.)

**Consortium of Aquariums, Universities, and Zoos**
Department of Psychology
California State University, Northridge
18111 Nordhoff St.
Northridge, CA 91330

**Friends of the National Zoo**
National Zoological Park
Washington, DC 20008
nationalzoo.si.edu

# 8

# Path 3: Aquatic Scientists

So, you want to work with dolphins or whales? In this chapter you'll learn how to go about it. But aquatic science offers much more than just working with marine mammals. Although aquatic science can be categorized as a subfield under botany (for the study of aquatic plant forms) or zoology (for the study of aquatic animals), and because it's a very popular and broad field, it can be looked at as a separate career path and deserves its own chapter.

Even so, *aquatic science* is still just a general term that encompasses several other fields and career paths. In fact, many universities offer separate programs or departments in the various aspects of aquatic science. Let's take a look at the options.

## Definition of the Career Path

*Aquatic science* is the general term for research conducted in oceans and coastal or inland waters connected to the sea. It is the study of the planet's aboveground waters and includes both salt- and freshwater environments.

Aquatic scientists study virtually everything having to do with water. For example, aquatic chemists research organic, inorganic, and trace-metal chemistry. Marine geologists study how ocean basins were formed and how geothermal and other geological processes interact with seawater. Freshwater geologists may study past climates or the organisms found in the sediments.

Aquatic scientists could also study processes that cover time scales ranging from less than a second to millions of years. They may also examine activity in spaces ranging from millimeters to oceanwide.

Aquatic science is interdisciplinary. While most aquatic scientists generally specialize in just one area, they use information from all fields and often work together with other scientists in teams or groups. For example, chemists and biologists might work together to understand the ways in which the chemical components of water bodies interact with plants, animals, and microorganisms such as bacteria.

## Oceanography

Oceanography is the specific study of the biological, chemical, geological, optical, and physical characteristics of oceans and estuaries. *Oceanographer* is a term that is usually understood to include ocean scientists, ocean engineers, and ocean technicians.

Ocean scientists investigate how the oceans work. They usually have a graduate degree in oceanography with a bachelor's degree in one of the fundamental science fields such as biology, physics, chemistry, or geology.

Ocean engineers perform the usual tasks of any engineers—such as designing a structure, for example—but they deal with specific issues related to that structure and its environment in the sea. For example, an ocean engineer might design supports for oil-well drilling equipment that would stand on the ocean floor. They would have to take into account information about ocean currents and the force the currents would exert on the structure, plus saltwater corrosion, marine life interference, and other similar elements. Ocean engineers also design the equipment oceanographers use to make oceanographic measurements.

Ocean technicians are responsible for equipment calibration and preparation, measurements, sampling at sea, instrument maintenance and repair, and data processing. Ocean technicians usually have a bachelor's degree, although some may be successful at finding work with two-year associate's degrees.

The subfields of oceanography are physical oceanography, chemical oceanography, biological oceanography, and geological and geophysical oceanography.

Physical oceanographers study currents, waves, and motion and the interaction of light, radar, heat, sound, and wind with the sea. They are also interested in the interaction between the ocean and atmosphere and the relationship among the sea, weather, and climate. Chemical oceanographers study chemical compounds and the many chemical interactions that occur in the ocean and on the ocean floor.

Biological oceanographers are interested in describing the diverse life-forms in the sea, their population densities, and their natural environment. They try to understand how these animals and plants exist in interrelationships with other sea life and substances and also focus on the impact of human intervention on the oceanic environment. Geological and geophysical oceanographers study the shape and nature and origin of the material of the seafloor.

### Limnology

Limnology involves the same concerns that oceanography studies but is limited to inland systems such as lakes, rivers, streams, ponds, and wetlands, and includes both fresh and salt water. Physical limnologists study water movements. Optical limnologists study the transmission of light through the water.

### Marine Biology Science

Marine biology or science refers specifically to the sea—saltwater environments—and covers a surprising variety of disciplines. Examples include planetology, meteorology, physics, chemistry, geology, physical oceanography, paleontology, and biology. Marine science also includes archaeology, anthropology, sociology, engineering, and other studies of human relationships with the sea.

Biologists study living things and their interaction with each other and the environment. Some study single species, others may examine how two or more species interact, and still others seek to understand the workings of an entire ecosystem.

Marine mammal science (yes, the study of dolphins and whales) covers about one hundred species of aquatic or marine mammals that depend on fresh water or the ocean for part or all of their lives. The species include pinnipeds, which cover seals, sea lions, fur seals, and walrus; cetaceans, which include baleen and toothed whales, ocean and river dolphins, and porpoises; sirenians, which cover manatees and dugongs; and some carnivores, such as sea otters and polar bears.

Marine mammal scientists work to understand these animals' genetic, systematic, and evolutionary relationships; population structure; community dynamics; anatomy and physiology; behavior and sensory abilities; parasites and diseases; and geographic and microhabitat distributions. Marine mammal scientists also study ecology, management, and conservation.

## Possible Employers

Aquatic scientists find employment in universities and colleges. They also work for international organizations, federal and state agencies, private companies, nonprofit laboratories, and local governments, or aquariums, zoos, marine parks, and museums. They also may be self-employed.

Government agencies that hire aquatic scientists include:

| | |
|---|---|
| Army Corps of Engineers | National Oceanic and Atmospheric |
| Coast Guard | Administration |
| Departments of Commerce, | National Park Service |
| Energy, Interior, Navy, and | National Science Foundation |
| State | Naval Oceanographic Office |
| Environmental Protection Agency | Naval Research Laboratory |
| Marine Mammal Commission | Office of Naval Research |
| Minerals Management Service | Smithsonian Institution |
| National Aeronautics and Space | U.S. Fish and Wildlife Service |
| Administration | U.S. National Biological Service |
| National Marine Fisheries Service | U.S. Navy, Office of Naval Research |

Private industries such as oil and gas exploration, production, and transportation as well as commercial fishing hire aquatic scientists when their operations affect marine mammals or produce environmental concerns. Many environmental, advocacy, and animal welfare organizations as well as legal firms also depend on aquatic scientists and use them for legal/policy development, problem solving, and regulatory and administrative roles.

Aquariums, marine parks, and zoos hire specialists for veterinary care, husbandry, training, research, and education programs. Examples of marine mammal jobs include researcher, field biologist, fishery vessel observer, laboratory technician, animal trainer, animal care specialist, veterinarian, whale-watch guide, naturalist, and educator.

Museums hire specialists for research, educational programs, and curatorial positions. Magazines, book publishers, television, and radio also provide employment for specialists, but usually on a part-time, freelance, or consulting basis.

## Training and Qualifications

There are a few entry-level positions here and there for people with only high school diplomas, but these positions are rare and opportunities for career advancement would be limited. Most entry-level jobs require a bachelor's degree in a natural science from an accredited college or university. Because most bachelor degree programs do not usually require research experience, applicants may expect to participate as assistants in research and advance mostly on the basis of on-the-job experience.

A master's degree is required by many employers, especially where research is a large part of the job description. A doctorate is usually necessary for academic positions or in other settings where the employee manages other scientists and conducts studies of his or her own design. Job opportunities are varied and exist at all educational levels. As with other fields, the higher-level and better-paying jobs require the most education.

Because aquatic science encompasses so many specializations, at the undergraduate level future biologists should obtain the broadest education possible. There is no guarantee you will gain employment in your area of interest or specialization—at least not right away. A general education will provide a foundation for many types of employment. Aquatic scientists usually acquire a foundation in one or more of the basic sciences such as biology, chemistry, geology, mathematics, or physics before specializing.

Many of the disciplines in aquatic science, such as marine biology, are graduate-level pursuits, so when choosing your undergraduate program, it's a good idea to investigate the strengths and specializations of the biology programs. If you know you want to pursue graduate work in marine science, for example, then taking your undergraduate degree at a university that offers courses in that area will help when it comes time to apply to graduate school. But graduate schools prefer students to major in a core science such as biology, physics, chemistry, or geology rather than a specialized subject such as limnology or oceanography. You can specialize in the areas that interest you the most, but not exclusively. Make sure to add statistics, mathematics, computers, and data management to your curriculum. And as in any profession, good oral and writing skills are crucial.

To increase your employability, involvement in a research project in a science laboratory is also important. This might be pursued through your university as a supervised independent study, working with a particular professor's research project, or through an internship, work-study job, or a stint of volunteering. If your university doesn't offer opportunities in this area, seek out other aquatic scientists, perhaps working at a local aquarium or marine science center and volunteering to help in any way you can.

In addition, many summer research programs are available at universities with graduate-level limnology or oceanography programs. These summer research experiences are usually offered to students after they have completed their sophomore or junior year and offer a good chance to learn more about the discipline as a possible career choice. You can find out about these programs by writing to institutions offering graduate degrees in limnology or oceanography. The programs are open to students from all universities.

To further prepare yourself, you can attend seminars and join aquatic science organizations such as the American Society of Limnology and Oceanography. (Their address is provided at the end of this chapter.) By doing so you will better understand the field and start making contacts in the community of people with whom you'll eventually work. Note that many careers in marine mammal science require additional qualifications such as scuba certification and boat-handling experience.

To summarize, make sure you acquire an all-around education and are familiar with what's happening in aquatic science. Get involved, talk to scientists, and participate in any way you can.

## Finding an Aquatic Science Program

Information on colleges and universities offering programs in aquatic science and all its subfields can be found through various directories such as Lovejoy or Peterson, available at school guidance centers, public libraries, or on the Internet.

You will find the programs listed under various headings such as:

| | |
|---|---|
| Aquatic science | Marine biology |
| Biology | Meteorology |
| Chemistry | Ocean engineering |
| Earth science | Oceanography |
| Geology | Physics |
| Limnology | |

## Career Outlook

In general, opportunities are good for those with bachelor's degrees or higher in science. But some specialty areas present stiff competition to job applicants. For example, there may be ten thousand people who would like a job working with marine mammals but only around one hundred jobs in this area nationwide. That is one extreme. In other specializations, there may be only five jobs nationwide but only four qualified applicants.

Opportunities are best for those with strong training in mathematics or engineering and those who pursued an interdisciplinary program that will allow them to work across disciplines. Current environmental concerns should provide employment opportunities in areas such as global climate change, environmental research and management, fisheries science, and marine biomedical and pharmaceutical research programs. American students and scientists are also expected to become more involved in international research programs.

Even when the number of available positions in this career path is small, top scientists are always in demand. It is important to remember that job opportunities and openings in all fields change over time and can change quite quickly. If you follow your interests, work hard, make contacts, and don't give up, you'll find the job that you are looking for.

## Earnings

Aquatic scientists enter this field for the love of their work, not for the money. The salary you'll earn will depend in part on your educational background, experience, responsibilities, area of specialization, number of years of service, and the size, type, and geographic location of the employing institution. In general, jobs with the government or in industry have the highest pay.

Bachelor's degree holders with no experience may find employment with the federal government at GS-5 to GS-7, a salary range in the teens to the thirties. Doctorate degree holders generally earn from $30,000 to $80,000 per year, and sometimes more than $100,000 per year for senior scientists or full professors, but high competition in some areas will most likely keep salaries at a modest level. Examples of aquatic sciences that presently pay above-average salaries are physical oceanography, marine technology and engineering, and computer modeling.

Some aquatic scientists earn their incomes from more than one source. They teach at universities, for example, and supplement their incomes by obtaining research grants from the federal or state government or private sources, writing for technical publications, and serving as consultants.

## Working Conditions

Many aquatic science researchers spend time each year engaged in fieldwork, collecting data and samples in natural environments. The data are collected during research cruises on small or large vessels, and the amount of time at

sea could last from one week to over two months and involve a team of scientists from many disciplines. Limnological data most often are collected during short, one- to two-day field trips that are usually narrower in scope, or
at the other extreme, could involve stays at field stations lasting from days to
months.

When not in the field, aquatic research scientists spend most of their time
in the laboratory running experiments, or at the computer analyzing data or
developing models. They also study papers in scientific journals and relate
that research to their own work. Writing their own papers for publication is
also part of their routine; for many scientists this extends to writing research
proposals to obtain grant money for further research.

Those working in universities must couple lectures and student conferences with their own research. In any scientific environment, attending meetings is also part of the job.

For aquatic scientists with administrative jobs, time is spent in the office
or communicating with colleagues and the public. Like any research scientists, they also attend national or international conferences to keep up in their
fields.

Hands-on workers, such as those involved with marine mammals or working in aquariums, have jobs that are not as glamorous as movies or TV programs depict. The work involves hard labor, such as lugging buckets of fish
and cleaning tanks.

## Close-Ups

Following are descriptions of two positions at the New England Aquarium
in Boston, Massachusetts, one of the premiere showcases for the display of
marine life and habitats. Its mission is to "present, promote, and protect the
world of water." These goals are carried out through exhibits and through
education, conservation, and research programs. Exhibits showcase the diversity, importance, and beauty of aquatic life and habitats, and they also highlight aquatic conservation issues of importance.

The centerpiece of the aquarium is the 200,000-gallon Giant Ocean
Tank Caribbean Coral Reef exhibit, which rises through four stories of the
facility. Visitors are afforded a multi-angle view of sea turtles, sharks, moray
eels, and the tropical fish that live inside. The Ocean Tray, which holds
131,000 gallons of water and surrounds the Great Ocean Tank on the ground
floor, is home to a colony of blackfooted and rockhopper penguins.

The Giant Ocean Tank and the Ocean Tray are managed by Steven Bailey, curator of fishes at the aquarium. The curator of fishes is responsible for fishes, invertebrates, reptiles, amphibians, birds, and plants. Steven's staff of twenty-four people includes nineteen aquarists, four supervisors, and a curatorial associate.

The majority of Steven's responsibilities are administrative. He is in charge of hiring, which is a very selective process since two hundred applications are often received for one advertised position. He also deals with budget and personnel issues, and is therefore removed from much of the day-to-day work of his department. Given this aspect of the job, Steven states that "If I had taken accounting courses and abnormal psychology, I would be much more prepared for this particular position than with all the biology I studied."

Steven received his bachelor's degree in zoology from Wilkes University in Wilkes-Barre, Pennsylvania, and completed substantial work toward a master's degree in ichthyology at Northeastern University in Boston. His goal while in graduate school was to find a job that would allow him to pursue his childhood passion for diving. During four busy years in graduate school, Steven tried to gain as much experience as possible to ensure employment. He volunteered with the National Marine Fishery Service and spent time as a professional collector of specimens used for biomedical research.

A position as aquarist became available while Steven was volunteering at the New England Aquarium, and he was hired for that job. He advanced over thirteen years, spending ten years as an aquarist, then being promoted to senior aquarist. He bypassed the last step as supervisor and moved directly to his position as curator of fishes.

Steven Bailey's group controls eighty to ninety exhibits at the aquarium, from the 200,000-gallon Caribbean Reef exhibit to a 50-gallon sea horse and pipefish exhibit. In addition to caring for the animals, Steven says that maintaining these exhibits also involves "the 3 Ws—the aesthetics—the windows, the walls, and the water. They all have to be clean and aesthetically appealing so that when folks come to visit us they are immediately assured that professionals are managing the animals."

Although he did prefer being in the field to administrative work, Steven derives satisfaction and a sense of accomplishment from his involvement in the design and construction of exhibits. Husbandry workers, designers, educators, and researchers work together to plan exhibits for the coming years.

In contrast to Steven Bailey's administrative position, consider his earlier job as senior aquarist at the New England Aquarium. This position is currently held by Heather Urquhart, a certified advanced scuba diver who takes care of the Giant Ocean Tank and the penguin colony. She has a bachelor's degree in biology with a concentration in marine biology from Salem State College. Plans to study for a master's degree changed once Heather began working at the aquarium. As she says, "Once you get involved with your work doing something that you love, it's hard to break away to go back to school."

Heather volunteered at the aquarium while in college. After graduation, she worked with an environmental consulting firm and did quality-control work with seafood, she applied for every position that became available at the aquarium. She was hired in 1989 as an aquarist-in-training, then became an aquarist, and is now senior aquarist in the Fishes Department.

On a typical day, Heather dives into the tank up to five times in order to feed, examine, and check the health of the fish. She also cleans and maintains the exhibits. The penguin exhibit has a 150,000-gallon tank of fifty-five-degree water. Although the water is chest-deep, a wet suit is needed due to the low temperature.

This is a physically demanding job. Heather must get into her dive equipment, walk to the tank, and dive and perform her tasks in the exhibit. In addition, she carries two fifteen-pound buckets of fish up and down the stairs to the tank. While this might sound like a daunting chore, interaction with the animals makes it all worthwhile for Heather. She works mainly with the penguins, some of which she has hand-raised from egg to adult. Heather calls this interaction "some of the best medicine going. No matter what kind of aggravating day you might be having, when you are working with the animals, it all seems not to matter so much."

In addition to maintaining the exhibit, Heather has formed a conservation program for the endangered African penguin. Visitors donate fifty-one cents—fifty cents is kept for the conservation fund, and one penny goes through a machine that imprints it with an image of an African penguin. The fund gets a contribution and the visitor gets a souvenir. Heather has traveled to South Africa to work with conservation organizations. The aim of these trips is both to contribute to the conservation effort and to learn as much as possible about the penguins' plight.

The positions of Heather Urquhart and Steven Bailey offer a glimpse of the many job opportunities available at a facility like the New England Aquarium. For example, in a floating pavilion adjacent to the aquarium, sea lion presentations of natural and learned behaviors are featured every day. Harbor seals reside in the outdoor pool on the aquarium's plaza. Some of these seals were found as orphaned pups along the New England coast and have been cared for by skilled aquarium biologists as part of their Rescue and

Rehabilitation Program. Through this program, aquarium staff work with distressed or injured marine animals in the wild such as whales, dolphins, sea turtles, and seals. Their goals are to rescue, rehabilitate, and whenever possible release the animals back to the wild.

Other research programs include working to preserve the endangered red-bellied turtle species and helping to increase the declining population of blackfooted penguins. The aquarium also offers a whale-watch program and a "Science at Sea" harbor tour boat.

To maintain such a range of exhibits and programs, the New England Aquarium relies on the skills and experience of a variety of professionals. The jobs described in this section are just two of the many possible careers in aquatic biology.

---

### ADVICE FROM THE PROFESSIONALS

Steven Bailey offers this view of his profession: "It is a career for people who are very serious. There aren't that many opportunities, and you have to be really dedicated to this pursuit. Most of the folks here have not been hired right out of college. They spent a good deal of time volunteering at this institution and picking up a lot of other related work experiences, expanding their horizons, and becoming Renaissance-type people. The diversity of experiences that individuals can have is very important as far as making them attractive commodities when hiring time comes around. There are very few people here who were hired on their first go-round.

"This job requires that you have construction and tool skills. It demands you know your way around the literature or at least be able to find the information to answer a question or solve a problem. It requires an ability to be comfortable with routine and what can often become repetitive work.

"Being an aquatic chambermaid, which almost everyone is, might sound like fun, but when you are cleaning and maintaining an animal's environment day after day, it can get very old for some people. For other people it's a Zen experience. They put it into perspective; they are able to be at peace with the incredible amount of responsibility they have for all of these animals."

Heather Urquhart's advice is specific: "Volunteer, volunteer, volunteer. That's the best bet. Not only will the people who work at the institution get to know your work, but you'll get an idea of what you'd be getting into, too.

"The glamorous part is that you get to work with a lot of cute baby animals. The nonglamorous part is all that other stuff—being in a wet suit all day long,

---

*continued*

cold water, and smelling like fish by the end of the day. Ninety percent of working with animals is cleaning up after them. It's not for everyone.

"But if it is for you, then volunteering is the way to go. The vast majority of the people working here formerly volunteered here. We do pull from within our ranks.

"Also, make sure you go to school, but don't specialize too much early on. For the type of job I have, you'd need to have a biology or zoology degree, one of these general topics. Then if you get to do some volunteer work, you can see more clearly what area to focus on. You might decide you want to work in a lab or in education."

## Strategies for Finding the Jobs

A good source for job announcements is the personnel department of a specific government agency, private company, educational institution, museum, zoo, marine park, or aquarium. Many of the professional associations listed at the end of this chapter post job listings and offer helpful links to other resources.

### Networking

Although what you know is very important, who you know also helps. Many job openings are never announced officially but are filled by personal recommendations. Volunteers or interns at an organization already have a foot well placed in the door. A professor might recommend a graduate student he or she is supervising to a colleague. An informal interview at a scientific conference you attend could result in a job offer.

### Internet

More and more organizations post information and job openings on the Web. Fire up any search engine and type in key words such as *biology careers* or *jobs with marine mammals*, and you'll be surprised at the number of resources you'll find.

## Professional Associations

In addition to information and professional contacts, some professional associations offer grants, scholarships, and training opportunities.

**American Cetacean Society**
P.O. Box 1391
San Pedro, CA 90733-1391
E-mail: info@acsonline.org
acsonline.org

**American Fisheries Society**
5410 Grosvenor Lane
Bethesda, MD 20814
E-mail: main@fisheries.org
fisheries.org

**American Geophysical Union**
2000 Florida Ave. NW
Washington, DC 20009
agu.org

**American Society of Limnology
and Oceanography**
The Academy of Natural Sciences
Estuarine Research Center
10545 Mackall Rd.
St. Leonard, MD 20685
E-mail: secretary@aslo.org
aslo.org

**American Society of Mammalogists**
Visit the society's website for a complete list of granting agencies and
funding sources: mammalsociety.org.

**American Veterinary Medical Association**
1931 N. Meacham Rd., Suite 100
Schaumburg, IL 60173
E-mail: avmainfo@avma.org
avma.org

**American Zoo and Aquarium Association**
Executive Office and Conservation Center
8403 Colesville Rd., Suite 710
Silver Spring, MD 20910-3314
aza.org

**Consortium of Aquariums, Universities, and Zoos**
Department of Psychology
California State University, Northridge
18111 Nordhoff St.
Northridge, CA 91330

**Environmental Careers Organization**
179 South St.
Boston, MA 02111
eco.org

**European Association for Aquatic Mammals**
Sarkanniemi
33230 Tampere
Finland
eaam.org

**European Cetacean Society**
Beach Cottage
Long Rock, Penzance
Cornwall TR20 8JE
United Kingdom

**Gulf Coast Research Laboratory**
USM College of Marine Sciences
703 East Beach Dr. (39564)
P.O. Box 7000
Ocean Springs, MS 39566-7000
coms.usm.edu

**IEEE Oceanic Engineering Society**
Institute of Electrical and Electronics Engineers IEEE-USA
1828 L St. NW, Suite 1202
Washington, DC 10036-5104
E-mail: ieeeusa@ieee.org
ieee.org

**International Association for Aquatic Animal Medicine**
Please visit the association's website for information: iaaam.org.

**International Marine Animal
Trainers Association**
1200 S. Lake Shore Dr.
Chicago, IL 60605

**Marine Technology Society**
5565 Sterrett Place #108
Columbia, MD 21044
E-mail: mtspubs@aol.com
mtsociety.org

**Minority Institutions Marine Science Association**
Department of Biology
Box 8540
Jackson State University
Jackson, MS 39217
jsums.edu/~marine

**National Oceanic & Atmospheric Administration**
14th St. & Constitution Avenue NW, Room 6217
Washington, DC 20230
noaa.gov

**National Sea Grant Office**
NOAA/Sea Grant, R/SG
1315 East-West Highway
SSMC-3, 11th Floor
Silver Spring, MD 20910
nsgo.seagrant.org

**The Oceanography Society**
P.O. Box 1931
Rockville, MD 20849-1931
E-mail: info@tos.org
tos.org

**Society for Marine Mammalogy**
Please visit the society's website for information regarding grants-in-aid and
links to other organizations: marinemammalogy.org.

**The Student Conservation
  Association**
Resource Assistant Program
689 River Rd.
P.O. Box 550
Charlestown, NH 03603-0550
thesca.org

**Technical Committee on
  Acoustical Oceanography**
Acoustical Society of America
2 Huntington Quadrangle, Suite 1N01
Melville, NY 11747-4502
E-mail: asa@aip.org
http://asa.aip.org

**Women's Aquatic Network**
P.O. Box 4993
Washington, DC 20008
E-mail: info@womensaquatic.net
womensaquatic.net

## Selected Internships
**Aquarium for Wildlife Conservation**
West 8th St. & Surf Ave.
Brooklyn, NY 11224
nyaquarium.com

**Aquarium of Niagara Falls**
Intern/Volunteer Program
701 Whirlpool St.
Niagara Falls, NY 14301-1094
niagarafallslive.com

**Belle Isle Zoo & Aquarium**
Intern/Volunteer Program
P.O. Box 39
Royal Oak, MI 48068-0039

**Center for Coastal Studies**
Intern Review Committee
Box 1036
Provincetown, MA 02657
E-mail: ccs@coastalstudies.org
coastalstudies.org

**Center for Marine
    Conservation**
The Ocean Conservancy
Intern/Volunteer Program
1725 DeSales St. NW, Suite 600
Washington, DC 20036
oceanconservancy.org

**Cetacean Research Unit**
Whale Center of New England
Intern/Volunteer Program
P.O. Box 159
Gloucester, MA 01931-0159
whalecenter.org

**Chicago Zoological Park**
Brookfield Zoo
Intern/Volunteer Program
3300 Golf Rd.
Brookfield, IL 60513
brookfieldzoo.org

**Clearwater Marine Aquarium**
249 Windward Passage
Clearwater, FL 33767-2244
cmaquarium.org

**Dolphins Plus**
P.O. Box 2728
Key Largo, FL 33037
pennekamp.com/dolphins-plus

**Florida Department of
    Environmental Protection**
Florida Marine Research Institute
Intern/Volunteer Program
100 8th Ave. SE
St. Petersburg, FL 33701-5095
floridamarine.org

**Friends of the National Zoo**
Research Traineeship Program
National Zoological Park
Washington, DC 20008
nationalzoo.si.edu

**John G. Shedd Aquarium**
Internship Coordinator
1200 S. Lake Shore Dr.
Chicago, IL 60605
sheddnet.org

**Kewalo Basin Marine Mammal
    Laboratory**
Intern Coordinator
1129 Ala Moana Blvd.
Honolulu, HI 96814
dolphin-institute.org

**Marine Mammal Research**
EPCOT Center, The Living Seas
Walt Disney World Company
P.O. Box 10000
Lake Buena Vista, FL 32830-1000

**Marine Mammal Research Program**
Intern/Volunteer Program
Texas A&M University at Galveston
Department of Fisheries and Wildlife
4700 Ave. U
Building 303
Galveston, TX 77551
tamug.edu/mmrp

**Mirage Hotel**
Intern/Volunteer Program
P.O. Box 7777
Las Vegas, NV 89177-0777

**Mote Marine Laboratory**
Intern/Volunteer Services
1600 Thompson Parkway
Sarasota, FL 34236
mote.org

**Mystic Marinelife Aquarium**
Intern/Volunteer Program
55 Coogan Blvd.
Mystic, CT 06355-1997
mysticaquarium.org

**National Aquarium in Baltimore**
Pier 3
501 E. Pratt St.
Baltimore, MD 21202-3194
aqua.org

**National Museum of Natural History**
Office of Education
P.O. Box 37012
Washington, DC 20560-0158
mnh.si.edu/edu_resources.html

**New England Aquarium**
Intern/Volunteer Program
Central Wharf
Boston, MA 02110
neaq.org

**The Oceania Project** (humpback whale research)
P.O. Box 646
Byron Bay
New South Wales 2481
Australia
oceania.org

**Pacific Whale Foundation**
Intern/Volunteer Program
300 Maalaea Rd., Suite 211
Wailuku, HI 96793
E-mail: programs@pacificwhale.org
pacificwhale.org

**Pinniped Learning & Behavior Project**
Long Marine Lab
Institute of Marine Sciences
University of California
1156 High St.
Santa Cruz, CA 95064
http://iims.ucsc.edu

**Tethys Research Institute**
c/o Municipal Aquarium
Viale G.B. Gadio 2
1-20121 Milan, Italy
tethys.org

**Theater of the Sea**
Intern/Volunteer Program
84721 Overseas Highway
Islamorada, FL 33036
theaterofthesea.com/intern.html

**Waikiki Aquarium**
Intern/Volunteer Program
University of Hawaii
2777 Kalakaua Ave.
Honolulu, HI 96815
http://waquarium.otted.hawaii.edu

**Whale Museum**
Volunteer Coordinator
62 First St. N
P.O. Box 945
Friday Harbor, WA 98250
whalemuseum.org

**Whale Research Group**
230 Mount Scio Rd.
Memorial University of
Newfoundland
St. John's, NF
Canada A1C 5S7
http://play.psych.mun.ca/psych/whale.html

## Field Programs (Pay to Volunteer)
**Cetacean Behavior Lab Internships**
Department of Psychology
College of Sciences
San Diego State University
5500 Campanile Dr.
San Diego, CA 92182
sci.sdsu.edu/cbl

**Coastal Ecosystems
Research Foundation**
P.O. Box 124
Port Hardy, BC
Canada V0N 2P0
E-mail: info@cerf.bc.ca
cerf.bc.ca

**EarthWatch International**
3 Clock Tower Place, Suite 100
Box 75
Maynard, MA 01754
earthwatch.org

**Green Volunteers**
1 Greenleaf Woods Dr., #302
Portsmouth, NH 03810
E-mail: info@greenvolunteers.com
greenvol.com
Offers a guide listing hundreds of volunteer opportunities worldwide,
including many marine mammal projects, for $22.00 including postage.
Short- and long-term opportunities available. Some projects require a
financial contribution.

**Mingan Island Cetacean Study**
285 Green St.
St. Lambert, QC
Canada J4P 1T3
rorqual.com

**Oceanic Society Expeditions**
Fort Mason Center
San Francisco, CA 94123
oceanic-society.org

**School for Field Studies**
10 Federal St.
Salem, MA 01970
fieldstudies.org

**University Research Expedition Programs**
University of California, Davis
One Shields Ave.
Davis, CA 95616
urep.ucdavis.edu

# 9

# Path 4: Medical Scientists, Technologists, and Technicians

If you always pictured yourself in a white lab coat or are fascinated by the idea of making new discoveries—cures for cancer or AIDS, for example—this may be the career path for you. But even if you prefer to work with proven methods and have some patient contact, a medical scientist or clinical technician career path could fill the bill.

## Definition of the Career Path: Medical Scientists

Biological scientists who do biomedical research are usually called medical scientists. Medical scientists working on basic research into normal biological systems often do so in order to understand the causes of and to discover treatment for disease and other health problems. Medical scientists may try to identify the kinds of changes in a cell, chromosome, or even the gene that signals the development of medical problems such as different types of cancer. After identifying structures of or changes in organisms that provide clues to health problems, medical scientists may then work on the treatment of problems. For example, a medical scientist involved in cancer research might try to formulate a combination of drugs that will lessen the effects of the disease. Medical scientists who have a medical degree might then administer the drugs to patients in clinical trials, monitor their reactions, and observe the results. (Medical scientists who do not have a medical degree normally collaborate with a medical doctor who deals directly with patients.) The medical scientist might then return to the laboratory to examine the results and, if necessary, adjust the dosage levels to reduce negative side effects or to try to induce even better results.

In addition to using basic research to develop treatments for health problems, medical scientists attempt to discover ways to prevent health problems from developing, such as affirming the link between smoking and increased risk of lung cancer, or alcoholism and liver disease. Most medical scientists specialize in some area of biology, such as microbiology or biochemistry.

Following are definitions for many of the areas of specialization:

Anatomists study the form and structure of animal bodies and try to determine the ability of animal bodies to regenerate destroyed or injured parts. They also investigate the possibility of transplanting whole organs or tissue fragments, such as skin.

Biochemists study the chemical composition of living things. They try to understand the complex chemical combinations and reactions involved in metabolism, reproduction, growth, and heredity. Biochemists may investigate causes and cures of diseases, or study the effects of food, hormones, or other substances on various organisms. Much of the work in biotechnology is done by biochemists and molecular biologists because this technology involves understanding the complex chemistry of life.

Biomedical engineers research and develop new ways to help people who are handicapped by the malfunction of a body organ. Biomedical engineers have created devices such as artificial hearts, kidneys, limbs, and joints.

Biophysicists study the physical principles within living cells and organisms. These scientists specialize in issues such as how the eye converts light into a signal to the brain or how radiation affects living matter.

Biotechnology is continually spurred by advances in basic biological knowledge, especially at the genetic and molecular levels. Biological and medical scientists use this technology to manipulate the genetic material of animals or plants, attempting to make organisms more productive or disease-resistant. The first application of this technology has been in the medical and pharmaceutical areas. Many substances not previously available in large quantities are starting to be produced by biotechnological means; some may be useful in treating cancer and other diseases.

Cellular biologists look at the organs and cells of the body by manipulating samples of cells with drugs or by physical means to see how they react under certain conditions. Developmental biologists, formerly known as embryologists, study the development of an animal from a fertilized egg through the hatching process or birth. They also study causes of healthy and abnormal development. Epidemiologists study the patterns of disease within a population. They also investigate how diseases are caused and how they spread. Geneticists study how different traits and disorders are inherited. They may also investigate methods for altering or producing new traits.

Immunologists study how the body protects itself against foreign invaders such as parasites, viruses, and transplanted organs. They research ways to develop vaccines to protect against disease and medicines to cure or prevent allergic reactions.

Microbiologists investigate microscopic organisms such as bacteria, viruses, algae, yeasts, and molds. These scientists try to discover how such organisms affect animals, plants, and the environment. Some microbiologists specialize in medicine or agriculture, while others focus on particular organisms. Microbiology includes virology and bacteriology.

Molecular biologists are interested in large molecules (usually DNA or protein), with the ultimate goal of discovering what they do in the animal. Advances in molecular biology have led to industrial spin-offs such as DNA fingerprinting and the manufacture of genetically engineered drugs and diagnostic tools.

Mycologists perform experiments on fungi to discover any that might be harmful to humans or could be useful to medicine, agriculture, and industry for the development of drugs, medicines, molds, and yeasts.

Pathologists study the nature, cause, and development of diseases and the changes to animals and plants caused by the diseases. They make diagnoses from body tissues, fluids, and other specimens. They also perform autopsies to determine the nature and extent of disease as well as the cause of death.

Pharmacologists develop new or improved drugs or medicines. They also conduct experiments to discover the effects of different drugs—the benefits and possible shortcomings or undesirable side effects.

## Definition of the Career Path: Clinical Technicians and Technologists

Clinical laboratory testing plays a crucial role in the detection, diagnosis, and treatment of disease. Clinical laboratory technologists and technicians, also known as medical technologists and technicians, perform most of these tests.

Clinical laboratory personnel examine and analyze body fluids, tissues, and cells. They look for bacteria, parasites, or other microorganisms; analyze the chemical content of fluids; match blood for transfusions; and test for drug levels in the blood to show how a patient is responding to treatment. They also prepare specimens for examination, count cells, and look for abnormal cells.

They use automated equipment and instruments that perform a number of tests simultaneously, as well as microscopes, cell counters, and other kinds of sophisticated laboratory equipment to perform tests. Then they analyze the results and relay them to physicians.

Some medical and clinical laboratory technologists supervise medical and clinical laboratory technicians. Technologists in small laboratories perform many types of tests, while those in large laboratories generally specialize.

Following are definitions for some of the specializations:

Blood bank technologists collect, type, and prepare blood and its components for transfusions. Clinical chemistry technologists prepare specimens and analyze the chemical and hormonal contents of body fluids. Cytotechnologists prepare slides of body cells and microscopically examine these cells for abnormalities that may signal the beginning of a cancerous growth. Immunology technologists examine elements of the human immune system and how it responds to foreign bodies. Microbiology technologists examine and identify bacteria and other microorganisms.

Medical and clinical laboratory technicians perform less complex tests and laboratory procedures than technologists. Technicians may prepare specimens and operate automatic analyzers, for example, or they may perform manual tests following detailed instructions.

Like technologists, they may work in several areas of the clinical laboratory or specialize in just one. For example, histology technicians cut and stain tissue specimens for microscopic examination by pathologists, and phlebotomists draw and test blood. They usually work under the supervision of medical and clinical laboratory technologists or laboratory managers.

## Possible Job Titles

Within this broad career path biology majors can use their undergraduate degrees as a stepping-stone to advanced medical training as physicians, nurses, physical therapists, and the wide spectrum of other practitioners who work with patients.

In addition to the definitions of the professional job titles just examined, here is a list of possible job titles that biology majors with additional training can pursue in the health-care fields:

| | |
|---|---|
| Audiologist | Dietitian |
| Biomedical engineer | Emergency medical technician |
| Chiropractor | Genetic counselor |

continued

| | |
|---|---|
| Hospital administrator | Phlebotomist |
| Industrial hygienist | Physical therapist |
| Medical records librarian | Physician in specialty areas |
| Nurse | Radiologic technologist |
| Occupational therapist | Recreational therapist |
| Ophthalmologist | Speech pathologist |
| Pharmacist | Veterinarian |

## Possible Job Settings

Many medical scientists are employed by county, state, and federal agencies or in the private sector with animal vaccine supply companies, clinical reference laboratories that do tests for physicians and health departments, and pharmaceutical corporations, as well as by hospitals, blood banks, and colleges and universities.

Many industries require the expertise of scientists to ensure the safety of their products, such as the cosmetics industry, food processing, and the dairy industry. Environmental and pollution control companies and the biotechnology industry also are large employers of biological scientists.

Some medical scientists work in management or administration or are employed as consultants to business firms or to government. They may plan and administer programs for testing foods and drugs, for example, or write for technical publications. Some medical scientists work in sales and service jobs for companies manufacturing chemicals or other technical products.

Almost one in four nonfaculty biological scientists is employed by federal, state, and local governments. Federal biological scientists work mainly in the U.S. Departments of Agriculture, the Interior, and Defense, and in the National Institutes of Health. Most of the rest work in the drug industry, which includes pharmaceutical and biotechnology establishments; hospitals; or research and testing laboratories.

More than half of employed clinical technologists and technicians work in hospitals. Most others work in medical laboratories and offices and clinics of physicians. Some work in blood banks, research and testing laboratories, and in the federal government at Department of Veterans Affairs hospitals and U.S. Public Health Service facilities.

## Training and Qualifications

The complexity of tests performed, the level of judgment needed, and the amount of responsibility workers assume depend largely on the amount of education and experience they have. Many students planning to enter medical schools or dentistry or veterinary colleges will fulfill part of their entrance requirements by taking courses or even completing bachelor's degrees in biology and zoology.

An increasing number of research scientists have both M.D. and Ph.D. degrees. In recognition of this growing trend, many medical schools and universities offer integrated M.D.-Ph.D. programs.

In addition to these routes into health care, there are numerous positions available as technicians and technologists both in clinical and research laboratories. In many cases, it is possible to find employment as a biomedical technician with a bachelor's degree, but it should be noted that the operation of diagnostic equipment often requires training beyond a degree. A bachelor's degree in biological science can lead to a career as a science or engineering technician, or as a health technologist or technician.

A master's degree is sufficient for some jobs in applied research. Many jobs in industry, such as in management, inspection, sales, and service, are also available to the qualified holder of a master's degree.

For biological scientists, the Ph.D. degree generally is required for college teaching, for independent research, and for advancement to administrative positions. Biological scientists should be able to work independently or as part of a team and be able to communicate clearly and concisely, both orally and in writing. Much of the work of a biological scientist involves writing research reports and grant proposals, as well as presenting papers at seminars and possibly supervising a research team.

Some graduates with a bachelor's degree start as biological scientists in testing and inspection, or get jobs related to biological science such as technical salesperson or service representative. Some may work as research assistants.

Those in industry or a health-care institution who aspire to management or administrative positions should possess good business skills and be familiar with regulatory issues and marketing and management techniques. Toward this end, many training programs offer or require courses in management, business, and computer applications. A master's degree can be particularly useful in this case, to broaden the applicant's background to include both science and business.

Medical scientists who administer drug or gene therapy to human patients or who otherwise interact medically with patients (such as excising tissue or performing other invasive procedures) must have a medical degree. It is increasingly common for medical scientists to earn both Ph.D. and medical degrees.

In addition to their formal education, medical scientists are usually expected to spend several years in a postdoctoral position before they are offered permanent jobs. Postdoctoral work provides valuable laboratory experience, including experience with specific processes and techniques (such as gene splicing) that is transferable to other research projects later on. In some institutions, a postdoctoral position can lead to a permanent position.

The usual requirement for an entry-level position as a medical or clinical laboratory technologist is a bachelor's degree with a major in medical technology or in one of the life sciences. Universities and hospitals offer medical technology programs.

It is also possible to qualify through a combination of on-the-job and specialized training. Bachelor's degree programs in medical technology include courses in chemistry, biological sciences, microbiology, and mathematics, and specialized courses devoted to knowledge and skills used in the clinical laboratory. Master's degrees in medical technology and related clinical laboratory sciences provide training for specialized areas of laboratory work or teaching, administration, or research.

The Clinical Laboratory Improvement Act (CLIA) requires technologists who perform certain highly complex tests to have at least an associate's degree. For example, medical and clinical laboratory technicians generally have either an associate's degree from a community or junior college, or a certificate from a hospital, vocational or technical school, or from one of the armed forces. A few technicians learn on the job.

Nationally recognized accrediting agencies in the clinical laboratory sciences include the National Accrediting Agency for Clinical Laboratory Sciences (NAACLS) and the Accrediting Bureau of Health Education Schools (ABHES). The NAACLS fully accredits 621 programs and approves 72 that provide education for medical and clinical laboratory technologists, cytotechnologists, histologic technicians, specialists in blood bank technology, and medical and clinical laboratory technicians. The ABHES accredits training programs for medical and clinical laboratory technicians.

Some states require laboratory personnel to be licensed or registered. Information on licensure is available from state departments of health or boards of occupational licensing.

Certification is a voluntary process by which a nongovernmental organization, such as a professional society or certifying agency, grants recognition to an individual whose professional competence meets prescribed standards. Widely accepted by employers in the health industry, certification is a prerequisite for most jobs and often is necessary for advancement. Agencies that certify medical and clinical laboratory technologists and technicians include the Board of Registry of the American Society of Clinical Pathologists, the American Medical Technologists, the American Society for Clinical Laboratory Science, and the Credentialing Commission of the International Society for Clinical Laboratory Technology. These agencies have different requirements for certification and different organizational sponsors.

Clinical laboratory personnel need analytical judgment and the ability to work under pressure. Close attention to detail is essential because small differences or changes in test substances or numerical readouts can be crucial for patient care. Computer skills are essential given the widespread use of automated laboratory equipment. Manual dexterity and normal color vision are also highly desirable.

Technologists may advance to supervisory positions in laboratory work or become chief medical or clinical laboratory technologists or laboratory managers in hospitals. Manufacturers of home diagnostic testing kits and laboratory equipment and supplies seek experienced technologists to work in product development, marketing, and sales. Graduate education in medical technology, one of the biological sciences, chemistry, management, or education usually speeds advancement.

A doctorate is sometimes needed to become a laboratory director. However, federal regulation allows directors of moderately complex laboratories to have either a master's degree or a bachelor's degree combined with the appropriate amount of training and experience. Technicians can become technologists through additional education and experience.

## Career Outlook

Positions for biological and medical scientists are expected to increase at faster than the average rate of job growth through 2010. Despite this promising news, however, applicants with Ph.D. degrees can expect to meet considerable competition for positions in basic research. The federal government funds much basic research and development, including many areas of medical research. Recent budget cutbacks have led to smaller increases in federal basic research expenditures, further limiting the dollar amount of each grant, although the number of grants awarded remains fairly constant. In addition, the number of Ph.D. graduates continues to grow, causing even greater competition for fewer jobs. Many of these graduates are turning to applied research positions in private industry; if the trend continues, these jobs will also become more competitive.

However, the need for continued research is apparent as environmental and health concerns permeate public awareness and become policy issues. More biological scientists will be needed to determine the environmental impact of industry and government actions and to prevent or correct environmental problems. Expected expansion in research related to health issues such as AIDS, cancer, Alzheimer's disease, and the Human Genome Project should result in employment growth.

Although this field is competitive, biological and medical scientists are less likely to lose their jobs during recessions than are those in many other occupations because many are employed on long-term research projects. A recession could, however, influence the funding granted to new research projects and the renewal of existing projects, particularly in areas of risky or innovative research.

The outlook for graduates with bachelor's and master's degrees is promising through 2010. It is anticipated that science-related jobs in sales, marketing, and research management will be more plentiful than independent research positions. Growth is also anticipated for science technicians and health technologists and technicians.

The growth of biotechnology companies in the last two decades has led to rapid employment gains. As the number of new firms begins to stabilize, employment should slow somewhat. However, much of the basic biological research done in recent years has resulted in new knowledge, and biological and medical scientists will be needed to take this knowledge to the next stage so that gene therapies can be developed to treat diseases.

Pharmaceutical firms are expected to use more biotechnology techniques, thereby increasing employment opportunities for biological and medical scientists. Employment of clinical laboratory workers is expected to grow as fast as the average for all occupations through 2010, as population growth leads to increased laboratory testing and the development of new tests.

## Earnings

According to the National Association of Colleges and Employers, beginning salary offers in private industry in 2000 averaged $29,235 a year for bachelor's degree recipients in biological science, about $35,667 for master's degree recipients, and about $42,744 for doctoral degree recipients.

Median annual earnings for biological and life scientists were about $49,239 in 2000. For medical scientists, median annual earnings were about $57,156.

In the federal government in 2001, general biological scientists in nonsupervisory, supervisory, and managerial positions earned an average salary of $61,236; microbiologists averaged $67,835; physiologists $78,366; and geneticists $72,510.

Median annual earnings for medical and clinical laboratory technologists were $40,510 in 2000. The median for those working in hospitals was $40,840, in medical and dental laboratories $39,780, and in offices and clinics of medical doctors $38,850.

Median annual earnings for medical and clinical laboratory technicians were $27,540 in 2000. The median for those working in hospitals was $28,860, in colleges and universities $27,810, in offices and clinics of medical doctors $27,180, and in medical and dental laboratories $25,250.

## Working Conditions

Medical scientists generally work regular hours in offices or laboratories and usually are not exposed to unsafe or unhealthy conditions. But some do work with dangerous organisms or toxic substances in the laboratory, so strict safety procedures must be followed to avoid contamination. Medical scientists also spend time working in clinics and hospitals, administering drugs and treatments to patients in clinical trials.

Hours and other working conditions vary according to the size and type of employment setting, especially for technologists and technicians. In large hospitals or in independent laboratories that operate continuously, personnel usually work the day, evening, or night shift, and may work weekends and holidays. Laboratory personnel in small facilities may work on rotating shifts rather than on a regular shift. In some facilities, laboratory personnel are on call, available in case of an emergency, and work several nights a week or on weekends.

Clinical laboratory personnel are trained to work with infectious specimens. When proper methods of infection control and sterilization are followed, few hazards exist. Laboratories generally are well-lighted and clean; however, specimens, solutions, and reagents used in laboratories sometimes produce odors. Laboratory workers may spend a great deal of time on their feet.

# Close-Ups

Carla Lee Suson is a micro/molecular biologist who has worked as a research assistant and chemical technician for a medical school and a chemical company, both in Texas. She has been in the field since 1985 and started her first lab job in her last year of college.

She has a B.A. in molecular biology from the University of Texas, Dallas, at Richardson, Texas, and graduated in 1986. She has also taken some master's-level classes at Texas A&M University in Kingsville.

A lifelong interest in medicine and an aptitude for science led to Carla's decision to become a research scientist. Her college studies prompted an interest in working with microscopes, centrifuges, and lab equipment. To Carla, "The work was fun and fascinating."

Carla's career has included working as a tissue culture technologist, studying the cellular causes of arthritis and rheumatism. She has also used radiation labels to trace the amount of proteins in a cell. Carla is familiar with using column chromatography, radioimmunoassays, wet chemistry techniques, gas chromatography, and spectrometry.

Carla Lee Suson has worked on a variety of research projects in her position as micro/molecular biologist. A typical research project involves ongoing experiments, which are often repeated day after day. The laboratory work is repetitive, as some projects can involve up to a year of running similar experiments again and again. An experiment can take several days to complete, using different procedures and different equipment along the way. The resulting raw data must then be analyzed for meaning.

Working in a laboratory environment requires certain work habits. According to Carla, "A person has to have very good record-keeping ability and clean habits to be a success at this. Being even slightly dirty, or unaware of what you are doing, not only can ruin the experiments but can also create a health hazard." An experiment can involve one hundred tubes of solutions; a scientist must be meticulous about monitoring exactly what is in each tube for the experiment to succeed.

Working in a microbiology lab is not usually a nine-to-five job. Experiments must be conducted when the animals or cells are ready to be tested, and deadlines for grant applications and research papers occasionally increase the workload.

Despite the repetition and sometimes long hours, Carla finds great satisfaction in her work: "I love the experimenting because it is like figuring out a puzzle. . . . I also love the idea that I am making some small effort to change mankind or help it through knowledge. When a doctor receives an award or publishes a paper, even though you don't get public acclaim for it, the whole lab celebrates. Without your little contribution, the experiment would not have happened."

In contrast to Carla's position as a molecular biologist, consider the job of Sharon Grata, medical laboratory technician. Sharon works for Conemaugh Health Systems at Memorial Medical Center, western Pennsylvania's major trauma center and teaching hospital.

Sharon's interest in medicine led to a decision to work with the analysis of blood and body fluids after a friend's death from leukemia. She earned an associate's degree in education from Mount Aloysious College in Cresson, Pennsylvania, and is working toward a B.S. in medical technology at St. Francis College in Loretto, Pennsylvania. Sharon had one year of clinical medical technician training through Lee Hospital School in Johnstown, Pennsylvania, and is certified by the American Society of Clinical Pathology.

Sharon Grata is a generalist at the hospital, rotating through the laboratory departments of phlebotomy, hematology, chemistry, blood bank, urinalysis, and microbiology. In the hematology department she runs blood counts using a machine that counts the number of red and white cells in a cubic milliliter of a blood sample. Blood counts help detect the presence of diseases such as leukemia and infections like mononucleosis. In the chemistry lab, serum is studied to measure levels of glucose, sodium, potassium, and other enzymes to establish a patient's chemical profile. The urinalysis lab checks kidney function, among other things. This involves checking a specimen by machine as well as centrifuging the specimen and examining it under a microscope. In the microbiology lab, Sharon checks for bacterial infections throughout the body. This is where a swab of the throat or eye, for example, is planted on various media in petri dishes; the resulting bacterial colonies are then run through antibiotic sensitivity tests to determine which antibiotic will kill the bacteria.

Working as a laboratory technician in a hospital setting can be stressful. A typical day begins at 4:00 A.M. so that blood can be drawn before patients have breakfast or are transported to surgery or for other tests. Technicians are called to draw blood from patients who have been seriously injured or killed in accidents or violent crimes. There is also danger involved in working with body fluids. As Sharon states, "One wrong move, just a blink of an eye, and at any time the technician could become infected with a dangerous disease such as hepatitis or HIV. And the pay does not compensate for the risks involved."

Despite the stress, however, Sharon finds her work rewarding: "Is it worth it? Yes. There isn't a day that goes by that I don't wonder how I can handle another day of stress, but then I look into the eyes of the patients and realize they are why I come back. The gratitude in their eyes is worth it."

## ADVICE FROM THE PROFESSIONALS

Carla Lee Suson offers this advice for aspiring micro/molecular biologists:

"Take classes in computers, chemistry, and statistics, as well as your normal biology classes. The knowledge can only help you. There are growing new fields in biophysics, radiation physics, and computer theoretical biology—a very new field—that will need new people and are paying top salaries.

"Work in labs while in school as much as you can and get experience in many different lab techniques. When you get out of school, your experience will give you the edge over other applicants.

"Make great grades. Most college kids think that C is good enough. When you apply for any science-oriented job, they will take a close look at your school transcripts, even when you have ten years' experience in the field. Science work is one of the few professions that look at your academic record almost as much, if not more so, than your work experience. If they don't like the grades you made, they won't hire you. Bad grades will haunt you the rest of your life. The A student gets hired more quickly."

Sharon Grata's experience allows her to offer this advice for those interested in work as medical laboratory technicians:

"My advice for anyone interested in this field is to continue your education and go into a research lab. Hospital laboratories are gearing up for more automation over a human workforce. But the research part of the field is opening up more. Become a hematologist or a Ph.D. chemist or obtain a master's degree in microbiology.

"If you choose not to go for the higher level of education, then look into design and repair of robotic equipment that is making its way into the labs. And know computers inside and out."

# Professional Associations

**Accrediting Bureau of
  Health Education Schools
  (ABHES)**
7777 Leesburg Pike, Suite 730
Falls Church, VA 22043
E-mail: info@abhes.org
abhes.org

**American Association of
 Anatomists**
9650 Rockville Pike
Bethesda, MD 20814-3998
E-mail: exec@anatomy.org
anatomy.org

**American Association of
 Blood Banks**
8101 Glenbrook Rd.
Bethesda, MD 20814-2749
E-mail: aabb@aabb.org
aabb.org

**American Association of
 Immunologists**
9650 Rockville Pike
Bethesda, MD 20814
E-mail: infoaai@aai.faseb.org
aai.org

**American Dietetic Association**
ADA Foundation
216 W. Jackson Blvd.
Chicago, IL 60606
adaf.org

**American Medical Technologists**
710 Higgins Rd.
Park Ridge, IL 60068-5765
E-mail: mail@amt1.com
amt1.com

**American Physiological
 Society**
Membership Services Department
9650 Rockville Pike
Bethesda, MD 20814-3991
the-aps.org

**American Society for Biochemistry and Molecular Biology**
9650 Rockville Pike
Bethesda, MD 20814-3996
E-mail: asbmb@asbmb.faseb.org
asbmb.org

**American Society for Clinical Laboratory Science**
6701 Democracy Blvd., Suite 300
Bethesda, MD 20817
E-mail: ascls@ascls.org
ascls.org

**American Society for Clinical Pathology**
2100 W. Harrison St.
Chicago, IL 60612
E-mail: info@ascp.org
ascp.org

**American Society for Microbiology**
1752 N St. NW
Washington, DC 20036
asmusa.org

**American Society for Pharmacology and Experimental Therapeutics**
9650 Rockville Pike
Bethesda, MD 20814
E-mail: info@aspet.org
aspet.org

**American Society of Cytopathology**
400 W. 9th St., Suite 201
Wilmington, DE 19801
cytopathology.org

**Association for Professionals in Infection Control and Epidemiology**
1275 K St. NW, Suite 1000
Washington, DC 20005-4006
E-mail: apicinfo@apic.org
apic.org

**Biomedical Engineering Society**
8401 Corporate Dr., Suite 225
Landover, MD 20785
E-mail: info@bmes.org
bmes.org

**Biophysical Society**
9650 Rockville Pike
Bethesda, MD 20814
E-mail: society@biophysics.org
biophysics.org

**Biotechnology Industry Organization**
1225 Eye St. NW, Suite 400
Washington, DC 20005
bio.org

**Genetics Society of America**
See website for contact information.
genetics-gsa.org

**National Accrediting Agency for Clinical Laboratory Sciences**
8410 W. Bryn Mawr Ave., Suite 670
Chicago, IL 60631
E-mail: info@naacls.org
naacls.org
For a list of accredited and approved educational programs for clinical
laboratory personnel.

**Society for Developmental Biology**
9650 Rockville Pike
Bethesda, MD 20814-3998
sdb.bio.purdue.edu

**Society for Neuroscience**
11 Dupont Circle NW, Suite 500
Washington, DC 20036
E-mail: info@sfn.org
sfn.org

# 10

# Path 5: Biology Educators

Teaching is the career path of choice for many people who feel that their love and knowledge of biology are best expressed by sharing it and encouraging it in others. No matter the area of specialization—botany or zoology, microbiology or the medical sciences—there are qualities and skills that all teachers must possess. In addition to being knowledgeable in their subjects, the ability to communicate, inspire trust and confidence, and motivate students, as well as understand their educational and emotional needs, is essential for teachers. They also should be organized, dependable, and patient, as well as creative.

## Definition of the Career Path

There are many career paths an educator can take, many different age groups to work with, and many different settings to work in. For the purposes of this chapter we will look at the two most traditional teaching paths for biology majors: secondary school and college and university teaching. Alternative suggestions are given later in this chapter under "Possible Job Settings."

To understand fully the career path, though, we first must look at the role of a teacher. It is changing from that of a lecturer or presenter to one of a facilitator or coach. Interactive discussions and hands-on learning are replacing rote memorization, especially in the earlier grades. For example, rather than merely telling students about biology or mathematics, a teacher might ask students to help perform a laboratory experiment or solve a mathematical problem and then discuss how these apply to the real world.

As teachers move away from the traditional repetitive-drill approaches, they are using more props or manipulatives to help students understand abstract concepts, solve problems, and develop critical thought processes. For example, young children may be taught the concept of numbers or adding and subtracting by playing board games. As students get older, they may use more sophisticated materials such as tape recorders, science apparatus, or cameras.

Classes are becoming less structured, and students are working in groups to discuss and solve problems together. Preparing students for the future workforce is the major stimulus generating the changes in education. To be prepared, students must be able to interact with others, adapt to new technology, and logically think through problems. Teachers provide the tools and environment for their students to develop these skills.

## Secondary Education

Secondary school teachers help students delve more deeply into subjects introduced in elementary school and learn more about the world and about themselves. They specialize in a specific subject, such as biology, Spanish, mathematics, history, or art. They may teach a variety of related courses, for example, botany and zoology.

Teachers may use films, slides, overhead projectors, and the latest technology in teaching, such as computers, telecommunication systems, and video discs. Telecommunication technology can bring the rest of the world into the classroom. Through telecommunications, U.S. students can communicate with students in other countries to share personal experiences or research projects of interest to both groups. Computers are used in many classroom activities, from helping students solve math problems to learning English as a second language. Teachers must continually update their skills to use the latest technology in the classroom.

Teachers design their classroom presentations to meet student needs and abilities. They also may work with students individually. Teachers assign lessons, give tests, hear oral presentations, and maintain classroom discipline. Teachers observe and evaluate a student's performance and potential. Teachers increasingly are using new assessment methods, such as examining a notebook of a student's research progress, to measure student achievement. Teachers assess the results at the end of a learning period to judge a student's overall progress. They can then provide additional assistance in areas where a student needs help.

In addition to classroom activities, teachers plan and evaluate lessons, sometimes in collaboration with teachers of related subjects. They also prepare tests, grade papers, prepare report cards, oversee study halls and homerooms, supervise extracurricular activities, and meet with parents and school staff to discuss a student's academic progress or personal problems.

### College and University Teaching

College and university faculty teach and advise over 14 million full-time and part-time college students and play a significant role in our nation's research. They also study and meet with colleagues to keep up with developments in their field and consult with government, business, nonprofit, and community organizations.

Faculty generally are organized into departments or divisions, based on subject or field. They usually teach several different courses in their department: introduction to biology, zoology, oceanography, marine science, and animal behavior, for example. They may instruct undergraduate or graduate students, or both.

College and university faculty may give lectures to several hundred students in large halls, lead small seminars, and supervise students in laboratories. They also prepare lectures, exercises, and laboratory experiments, grade exams and papers, and advise and work with students individually.

In universities, they also counsel, advise, teach, and supervise graduate-student research. They may use closed-circuit and cable television, computers, videotapes, and other teaching aids.

Faculty keep abreast of developments in their fields by reading current literature, talking with colleagues, and participating in professional conferences. They also do their own research to expand knowledge in their fields and write about their findings in scholarly journals and books.

Most faculty members serve on academic or administrative committees that deal with the policies of their institution, departmental matters, academic issues, curricula, budgets, equipment purchases, and hiring. Some work with student organizations. Department heads generally have heavier administrative responsibilities.

The amount of time spent on each of these activities varies by individual circumstance and type of institution. Faculty members at universities generally spend a significant part of their time doing research; those in four-year colleges, somewhat less; and those in two-year colleges, relatively little. However, the teaching load usually is heavier in two-year colleges.

## Possible Job Titles

There is not a wide latitude in job titles for professional biology teachers. We often apply the term *teacher* to indicate professionals in elementary school as well as the professionals filling the top posts at colleges and universities. Despite the subject area, rank, or setting, the teaching role essentially remains the same. They are all, to some extent, teachers.

## Possible Job Settings

Here we will look at all the settings in which a biology teacher can be employed. Some settings will expect teachers to follow a traditional, basic biology curriculum; others will want the work to focus on a specialty area. For example, a botanist or horticulturist, while not certified to teach in a public school system, could happily find work for the Cooperative Extension Service, a garden center, or botanical garden. The qualifications you'll need will vary depending on the work setting. Each setting has its own requirements of and expectations for its teachers, but each provides an environment where biology majors dedicated to teaching can practice their art.

| | |
|---|---|
| Adult education centers | Garden centers/nurseries |
| Aquariums | Peace Corps |
| Botanical gardens | Private schools |
| Community centers | Public schools |
| Community colleges | Recreational centers |
| Cooperative Extension Service | Rehabilitation centers |
| Four-year colleges and universities | Zoos |

## Training and Qualifications

To work in most public school systems, a bachelor's degree with a teaching certification is required. In other settings, such as some community colleges and most four-year universities, postgraduate degrees are required.

### Secondary Schools

Aspiring secondary school teachers either major in biology as the subject they plan to teach while also taking education courses, or major in education and take biology courses as their subject.

### Alternative Teacher Certification

Many states offer alternative teacher certification programs for people who have college training in the subject they will teach but do not have the necessary education courses required for a regular certificate. Alternative certification programs were originally designed to ease teacher shortages in certain subjects, such as mathematics and science. The programs have expanded to attract other people into teaching, including recent college graduates and midcareer changers. In some programs, individuals begin teaching immediately under provisional certification. After working under the close supervision of experienced educators for one or two years while taking education courses outside school hours, they receive regular certification if they have progressed satisfactorily.

Under other programs, college graduates who do not meet certification requirements take only those courses that they lack and then become certified. This may take one or two semesters of full-time study.

Aspiring teachers who need certification may also enter programs that grant a master's degree in education, as well as certification. States also issue emergency certificates to individuals who do not meet all requirements for a regular certificate when schools cannot find enough teachers with regular certificates.

## Competency Testing

Almost all states require applicants for teacher certification to be tested for competency in basic skills such as reading and writing, teaching skills, or subject matter proficiency. Almost all require continuing education for renewal of the teacher's certificate. Some require a master's degree.

## Reciprocity

Many states have reciprocity agreements that make it easier for teachers certified in one state to become certified in another. Teachers may become board certified by successfully completing the National Board for Professional Teaching Standards certification process. This certification is voluntary but may result in a higher salary. Information on certification requirements and approved teacher training institutions is available from local school systems and state departments of education.

## Colleges and Universities

Most college and university faculty are in one of four academic ranks: professor, associate professor, assistant professor, or instructor. A small number are lecturers.

Most faculty members are hired as instructors or assistant professors. Four-year colleges and universities generally hire doctoral degree holders for full-time, tenure-track positions but may hire master's degree holders or doctoral candidates for certain disciplines or for part-time and temporary jobs.

Doctoral programs usually take four to seven years of full-time study beyond the bachelor's degree. Candidates usually specialize in a subfield of a discipline, for example, microbiology, entomology, or plant physiology, but also take courses covering the whole discipline. Programs include twenty or more increasingly specialized courses and seminars plus comprehensive examinations on all major areas of the field. They also include a dissertation, a report on original research to address some significant question in the field.

Students studying the sciences usually do laboratory work; in the humanities, they study original documents and other published material. The dissertation, done under the guidance of one or more faculty advisors, usually takes one or two years of full-time work.

### Advancement

With additional preparation and certification, teachers may become administrators or supervisors, although the number of positions is limited. In some systems, highly qualified, experienced teachers can become senior or mentor teachers, with higher pay and additional responsibilities. They guide and assist less experienced teachers while keeping most of their teaching responsibilities.

Some faculty, based on teaching experience, research, publication, and service on campus committees and task forces, move into administrative and managerial positions, such as departmental chairperson, dean, and president. At four-year institutions, such advancement requires a doctoral degree.

## Career Outlook

The overall outlook for careers in teaching is positive. The following is a look at the prospects for jobs in school systems and higher education.

### School Systems

Job opportunities for teachers over the next ten years should be excellent, mostly because of the large number of teachers expected to retire. Intense competition for good teachers is already under way among employers in many locations, with schools luring teachers from other states and districts with bonuses and higher pay.

The job market for teachers varies by school location and subject specialty. Many inner cities and rural areas have difficulty attracting enough teachers, so job prospects should be better in these areas than in suburban districts.

Currently, many districts have difficulty hiring qualified teachers in science, mathematics, and computer science.

Increasing enrollments of minorities, coupled with a shortage of minority teachers, should intensify efforts to recruit minority teachers. There should also be an increasing need for bilingual teachers.

The number of teachers employed also depends on state and local expenditures for education and enactment of legislation to increase the quality of education. Many states are implementing policies that will encourage more students to become teachers.

## Higher Education

Employment of college and university faculty is expected to increase faster than the national average for all occupations through the year 2010, due largely to the unexpected increase in the population of eighteen- to twenty-four-year-olds. Adults returning to college and an increase in the number of minority students will add to enrollments, and the demand for minority teachers will be high.

Welfare-to-work policies and the need for continuing education will create new openings, particularly at community colleges. In addition, the retirements of faculty hired in the 1960s and 1970s will increase the number of job openings. In contrast, the number of doctorate degrees awarded is projected to rise by only 4 percent through 2010, which is sharply lower than the increase over the previous decade. A surplus of Ph.D. candidates in recent years has contributed to intense competition for college faculty jobs.

Although the competition for jobs should ease somewhat, it will remain tight for those seeking tenure-track positions at four-year colleges and universities. Many of the available jobs are expected to be part-time or renewable term appointments. The best prospects will continue to be in the computer science, engineering, and business fields, in which jobs outside academia are plentiful. Vocational and technical education teachers are also in short supply in the computer, business, and health-related fields.

Distance learning, particularly over the Internet, is expected to create a number of new jobs for postsecondary teachers. Distance learning is increasingly used by those in rural areas and those with family responsibilities. Employers are expected to use distance learning as a way to enhance workers' skills, and the U.S. Army has announced plans to offer distance learning to its troops. The increasing demand will result in the need for more teachers of online classes, both at traditional colleges and at new online universities.

## Earnings

The following is a breakdown of recent earnings for teachers at various levels of the educational system.

### School Systems

According to the American Federation of Teachers, the estimated average salary of all public elementary and secondary school teachers in the 1999–2000 school year was $41,820. Public secondary school teachers averaged about $39,845 a year, while public elementary school teachers averaged $37,300. Private school teachers generally earn less than public school teachers.

In 1999, over half of all public school teachers belonged to unions—mainly the American Federation of Teachers and the National Education Association—that bargain with school systems over wages, hours, and the terms and conditions of employment.

In some schools, teachers receive extra pay for coaching sports and working with students in extracurricular activities. Some teachers earn extra income during the summer working in the school system or in other jobs.

### Higher Education

Earnings vary according to faculty rank and type of institution, geographic area, and field. According to a 1999–2000 survey by the American Association of University Professors, salaries for full-time faculty averaged $58,400. By rank, the average for professors was $76,200, associate professors $55,300, assistant professors $45,600, lecturers $38,100, and instructors $34,700.

Faculty in four-year institutions earn higher salaries, on the average, than those in two-year schools. In 1999–2000, salaries for faculty in private independent institutions averaged $66,300, in public institutions $57,700, and in religious-affiliated institutions $51,300.

In fields with high-paying, nonacademic alternatives—notably medicine and law but also engineering and business, among others—earnings exceed these averages. In others—such as the humanities and education—they are lower. Most faculty members have significant earnings in addition to their base salary from consulting, teaching additional courses, research, writing for publication, or other employment, both during the academic year and the summer.

Most college and university faculty enjoy some unique benefits, including access to campus facilities, tuition waivers for dependents, housing and travel allowances, and paid sabbatical leaves. Part-time faculty have fewer benefits than full-time faculty and usually do not receive health insurance, retirement benefits, or sabbatical leave.

## Working Conditions

The working environment for educators can vary greatly, depending on the level at which you teach. The following are descriptions of the working conditions you can expect at the high school and college level.

### Secondary Education

Secondary school teachers teach from five to seven periods in a day and have extracurricular responsibilities as noted earlier, such as coaching sports or chaperoning school outings. In some secondary schools—and the problem is not limited to just inner-city schools—maintaining discipline has become a weighty part of the teacher's role.

On the positive side, secondary school teachers may help shape a student's future and assist in choosing courses, colleges, and careers. Special education teachers may help students with their transition into special vocational training programs, colleges, or jobs.

Teachers also participate in education conferences and workshops. Many enjoy several weeks' vacation during the school year and two months off in the summer. Others, though, to supplement their incomes, will teach summer school or find other part-time summer work.

### College and University Teaching

College faculty generally have flexible schedules. They must be present for classes, which usually add up to twelve to sixteen hours a week, and for faculty and committee meetings. Most establish regular office hours for student consultations and assistance, usually three to six hours per week. Otherwise, they are relatively free to decide when and where they will work and how much time to devote to course preparation, grading papers and exams, study, research, and other activities.

They may work staggered hours and teach classes at night and on weekends, particularly those faculty who teach older students who may have full-time jobs or family responsibilities during the weekdays. They have even greater flexibility during the summer break and school holidays, when they may teach or do research, travel, or pursue nonacademic interests. Most colleges and universities have funds used to support faculty research or other professional development needs, including travel to conferences and research sites.

Part-time faculty generally spend less time on campus than full-time faculty since they usually don't have an office. In addition, they may teach at more than one college, requiring travel between their various places of employment.

Faculty may experience a conflict between their responsibilities to teach students and the pressure to do research. This may be a particular problem for young faculty seeking advancement. Increasing emphasis on undergraduate teaching performance in tenure decisions may alleviate some of this pressure, however.

## Close-Up

Michele Graham is a biology lecturer at Cal-State Hayward University in Hayward, California. She has a B.A. in printmaking from the California College of Arts and Crafts in Oakland, California. In 1984 she earned her M.S. in biology at Cal-State Hayward and in 1996 her Ph.D. at the University of California, Berkeley, in evolutionary biology and entomology. Michele's initial interest was in zoology, and her hope is to "make a difference in our culture's perception about other life-forms so that we and they might have a chance to survive our greed and misuse of the planet."

Finding a university position in California was difficult, since molecular biologists and biochemists were more in demand than evolutionary ecologists. Michele applied to over forty colleges and universities throughout the United States, and only four or five of the positions were exactly in her field. She eventually found her current position through contacts she made while studying at Hayward.

The primary responsibility of a college instructor is teaching. Most instructors are responsible for one or two courses for which they develop and write lectures, select textbooks, write syllabi, and in the case of biology, develop labs to go along with the course.

Research is the secondary responsibility of a college instructor. As Michele describes it, "Research brings recognition to the department and money to the university or college and so is considered important. As someone interested in science, it would be expected that you enjoy doing research." In some institutions, instructors write books, articles, and textbooks in lieu of research.

In junior colleges, teaching takes precedence and research is not expected of instructors.

Instructors also participate in faculty meetings and campus committees, and are involved in the general business of the institution. These are time-consuming responsibilities that Michele must fit into her teaching and research schedule.

On a typical day, Michele Graham might give a lecture, meet with one or two labs, and monitor research projects. In addition, she will meet with students who work with her, attend a departmental or committee meeting, work on lecture notes, and read newly published research papers.

Michele advises that in the early years of this career, an instructor should be prepared to work sixty to seventy hours each week. "During this time you are trying to do a lot of research in order to publish as many papers as possible by the time of your review for tenure. Once you have tenure, things calm down a bit. But this is a demanding way to make a living, so you need to really love it to make it worthwhile."

Michele finds great satisfaction in working with students, which is "wonderful, exciting, never boring, and always challenging." Combined with "playing with ideas," seeing how students grasp a new concept and begin to understand its many implications is very gratifying. In Michele's words, "It is awe inspiring. To be part of this process as a teacher is a privilege, and it is the part of my job that gives it real meaning."

---

### ADVICE FROM A PROFESSIONAL

Here is Michele Graham's advice to prospective college biology instructors:

"My advice to all is to do something you love, regardless of how much money you will earn or how feasible it seems, or how difficult to accomplish. Work takes up a lot of time and a lot of years, and if you don't get up every day to something you love doing, your life is going to be miserable. So, the greatest quality to possess is being in love with your job.

"Being a biologist will require that you get at least a master's degree. To teach in college, you have to get a Ph.D. This will require at least five additional years of college, but be forewarned, it is getting more difficult to get a Ph.D. because the requirements of the research are stiffer. So it may, and often does, take considerably longer than five years. Once you get into graduate school everything will flow from there."

## Strategies for Finding the Jobs

Check with your college career office. Career offices regularly receive mailings of job openings. You can also leave your résumé on file there. Prospective employers regularly contact college career offices looking for likely candidates.

Seek out all the newspapers in your area or in the geographic location in which you'd prefer to work. A trip to the library will reveal periodicals you might not have been aware of and will be less of a burden on your budget.

The Internet is an incredible source for job hunting. Use any of the search engines available to you and type in keywords such as "employment," "biology," "teaching," and "jobs." You will discover a wealth of information online—organizations, educational institutions, publications, and a wide variety of potential employers and job search services—most of which are available at no charge above the online time your Internet provider charges you.

Biology educators, especially those hoping to land a job with a zoo or botanical garden, will find internships and volunteering stints the most important keys to employment. These settings cry out for volunteer help, and internships can be arranged through your university. Once in the door, make yourself indispensable. When a job opening occurs, you'll be on the spot, ready to step in.

Walk right in, set your portfolio or résumé down on the appropriate desk, and you might find you have just landed yourself a job. This approach works best in adult education centers, community centers, and other related settings.

*The Chronicle of Higher Education* is a weekly publication available by subscription or in any library or your college placement office. This is the old standby for those seeking positions within two- and four-year colleges and universities.

For private schools particularly, both at home and abroad, placement agencies can provide a valuable source for finding employment. Some charge both the employer and the prospective employee a fee; others charge just one or the other.

## Related Occupations

Teaching requires a wide variety of skills and aptitudes, including a talent for working with people; organizational, administrative, and record-keeping abilities; research and communication skills; the power to influence, motivate, and train others; patience; and creativity.

Workers in other occupations requiring some of these aptitudes include counselors, librarians, education administrators, writers, consultants, lobbyists, policy analysts, employment interviewers, preschool workers, public relations specialists, sales representatives, social workers, and trainers and employee development specialists.

## Professional Associations

Information on careers in teaching science can be obtained from:

**Association for**
**Biology Laboratory Education**
Department of Ecology & Evolutionary Biology
University of California, Irvine
Irvine, CA 92697-2525
http://ecoevo.bio.uci.edu/

**National Science Teachers**
**Association**
1840 Wilson Blvd.
Arlington, VA 22201-3000
nsta.org

Information on teachers' unions and education-related issues may be obtained from:

**American Federation of Teachers**
555 New Jersey Ave. NW
Washington, DC 20001
aft.org

**National Education Association**
1201 16th St. NW
Washington, DC 20036
nea.org

A list of institutions with teacher education programs accredited by the National Council for Accreditation of Teacher Education can be obtained from:

**National Council for Accreditation of
    Teacher Education**
2010 Massachusetts Ave. NW, Suite 500
Washington, DC 20036-1023
E-mail: ncate@ncate.org
ncate.org

For information on voluntary teacher certification requirements, contact:

**National Board for Professional
    Teaching Standards**
1525 Wilson Blvd., Suite 500
Arlington, VA 22209
nbpts.org

For additional information contact:

**American Association for Higher Education**
One Dupont Circle, Suite 360
Washington, DC 20036-1143
E-mail: info@aahe.org
aahe.org

**American Association of Christian Schools**
P.O. Box 1097
Independence, MO 64051-0597
E-mail: national@aacs.org
aacs.org

**American Association of Colleges for Teacher Education**
1307 New York Ave. NW, Suite 300
Washington, DC 20005
aacte.org

**American Association of State
    Colleges and Universities**
1307 New York Ave. NW, 5th Floor
Washington, DC 20005
aascu.org

**Association for Childhood
Education International**
17904 Georgia Ave., Suite 215
Olney, MD 20832
E-mail: aceihq@aol.com
udel.edu/bateman.acei

**Council for American
Private Education**
13017 Wisteria Dr. #457
Germantown, MD 20874
E-mail: cape@capenet.org
capenet.org

**National Association for the
Education of Young Children**
1509 16th St. NW
Washington, DC 20036
naeyc.org

**National Association of
Independent Schools**
1620 L St. NW, Suite 1100
Washington, DC 20036-5695
nais.org

**Publications**
*The Chronicle of
Higher Education*
Circulation Department
1255 23rd St. NW
Washington, DC 20037
chronicle.com

*JCST*
National Science Teachers Association
1840 Wilson Blvd.
Arlington, VA 22201-3000
nsta.org

The *Journal of College Science Teaching* ( *JCST* ) is a refereed journal published by the National Science Teachers Association (NSTA) for an audience of college and university teachers of introductory and advanced science courses. *JCST* communicates innovative, effective techniques to improve interdisciplinary teaching strategies for instructing both science majors and nonmajors.

# Additional Resources

To complement the resources provided at the end of each chapter, listed below are additional publications, associations, and institutions to contact for more career or training information:

**American Society of Agronomy**
677 S. Segoe Rd.
Madison, WI 53711
E-mail: headquarters@agronomy.org
agronomy.org

**Institute of Food Technologies**
525 W. Van Buren, Suite 1000
Chicago, IL 60607
E-mail: info@ift.org
ift.org

**National Association of Science Writers**
P.O. Box 890
Hedgesville, WV 25427
nasw.org

## Additional Publications for Zoology Majors

The following publications offer additional information on career opportunities in zoology.

Carpenter, James W., Dr. *The Exotic Animal Formulary*. Available through Veterinary Specialty Products, Inc., P.O. Box 812005, Boca Raton, FL 33481. $29.95 plus $3.00 shipping.

The Center for Wildlife Law quarterly newsletter. (Visit the center's website at ipl.unm.edu/cwl.)

Kalamazoo Nature Center. *Wild Animal Care and Rehabilitation Manual*, 4th ed. Available through Kalamazoo Nature Center, 7000 N. Westnedge Ave., Kalamazoo, MI 49007.

Kyle, Georgean Z. and Paul D. *Housing Avian Insectivores During Rehabilitation*. Available through Driftwood Wildlife Association, P.O. Box 39, Driftwood, TX 78619.

Landau, Diana and Shelley Stump. *Living with Wildlife*. San Francisco: Sierra Club, 1994. (A good book for the general public; stresses who is qualified to care for injured and orphaned animals and also gives info on rehabilitation, permits, etc.)

Miller, Louise. *Careers for Animal Lovers and Other Zoological Types*, 2nd ed. Chicago: VGM Career Books, 2000.

Musgrave, Ruth S. and Maryann Stein. *State Wildlife Laws Handbook*. Albuquerque: The University of New Mexico Center for Wildlife Law, 1993.

National Wildlife Federation. *Conservation Directory*. Purchase online at nwf.org/conservationdirectory, or by mail from Island Press, P.O. Box 7, Covelo, CA 95248. $70.00 plus shipping.

Raley, Patti L. *Primer of Wildlife Care & Rehabilitation*. (Contains extensive diet information, lab techniques, veterinary info, charts with species info, etc.) Available through Brukner Nature Center, 5995 Horseshoe Bend Rd., Troy, OH 45373. $24.95 plus $2.00 shipping.

Rule, Marcy. *The Songbird Diet Index*. Available through Coconut Creek Publishing Co., 2201 N.W. 40th Terrace, Coconut Creek, FL 33066-2032. (Includes natural and rehabilitation diets for 149 bird species.) $23.00 plus shipping.

White, Jan. *Basic Wildlife Rehabilitation IAB*. Suisun, CA: International Wildlife Rehabilitation Council, 1993. (This is the manual that goes along with the Basic Wildlife Rehab. IAB skills seminar; contains medical and diet calculation information.)

*Wildlife Rehabilitation Today*. (Published quarterly.) Coconut Creek Publishing Company, 2201 N.W. 40th Terrace, Coconut Creek, FL 33066-2032. (Visit the website, wildliferehabtoday.com.)

Willowbrook Wildlife Haven. *Willowbrook Wildlife Haven Volunteer Handbook*. Available through Willowbrook Wildlife Haven, P.O. Box 2339, Glen Ellyn, IL 60138. (An excellent volunteer manual. Good for general

information as well as a model for volunteer manuals. Good species care
and natural history information.)

## Additional Resources for Aquatic Scientists

The following resources provide additional information on job opportunities
for aquatic scientists.

*The Chronicle of Higher Education* lists academic positions at junior colleges, colleges, and universities. Its address and information on obtaining academic positions are covered more fully in Chapter 10.

The American Geophysical Union, whose address is listed at the end of
this chapter, publishes *Eos*, a weekly newspaper that lists employment opportunities, particularly in government and universities (agu.org). Other technical journals carry similar postings.

Many manufacturing companies with significant interest in the oceans
advertise in Sea Technology (sea-technology.org). Other manufacturers, consulting firms, and universities that are potential employers are listed among
the corporate sponsors of the Marine Technology Society, and their names
are listed in each issue of the society's journal (mtsociety.org).

The following offer publications and information packets:

*Careers in Oceanography.* Available through the American Geophysical Union,
2000 Florida Ave. NW, Washington, DC 20009 (agu.org).
*Careers in Oceanography and Marine-Related Fields.* Available through The
Oceanography Society, P.O. Box 1931, Rockville, MD 20849-1931. To
view the booklet online, visit onr.navy.mil/onr/careers.
Earth Work Career Publications Service. SCA, Attn: Earth Work, P.O. Box
550, Charlestown, NH 03603. (Various publications on environmental
careers.)
Heitzman, William Ray. *Opportunities in Marine and Maritime Careers*, 2nd
ed. Lincolnwood, IL: VGM Career Books, 1999.
*Marine Education: A Bibliography of Educational Materials Available from the
Nation's Sea Grant College Programs.* Available through Sea Grant Marine
Education Bibliography, Michigan Sea Grant (miseagrant.org/pubs/mari-
need) ($2.00/copy).
*Marine Science Careers: A Sea Grant Guide to Ocean Opportunities.* Available
through Sea Grant Communications Office, University of New Hampshire, Kingman Farm, Durham, NH 03824-3512. Send $5.00 check
payable to University of New Hampshire.

*Ocean Opportunities—a Guide to What the Oceans Have to Offer.* Available through Marine Technology Society, 2000 Florida Ave. NW, Suite 500, Washington, DC 20009 ($3.00/copy).

*Sea Technology Buyer's Guide.* Contact Compass Publications, Inc., 1501 Wilson Blvd., Suite 1001, Arlington, VA 22209 (sea-technology.com) to receive this guide.

# Index